get an ethical life

Peter MacBride

flash.

For Nat,

who wanted to live a greener life

Hodder Education
338 Euston Road, London NW1 3BH.

Hodder Education is an Hachette UK company

First published in UK 2011 by Hodder Education.

British Library Cataloguing in Publication Data: a catalogue record for this title is available from the British Library.

10 9 8 7 6 5 4 3 2 1

www.hoddereducation.co.uk

Typeset by MPS Limited, a Macmillan Company.
Printed in Great Britain by CPI Cox & Wyman, Reading.

Contents

1

basic ethics

Ethical behaviour is that which is good, and we all have an inner voice which tells us what is good. And the basic principles of goodness remain the same, though how they are interpreted into actual behaviour does vary between cultures. An ethical person is one who has concern for the well being of others, and who is aware of the impact of their actions on others. It's in the second part of that – the awareness of impact – where even the best-intentioned of us can fail. On a personal level, we can act with concern for others in a range of ways, from doing good at one end of the scale, to avoiding doing harm at the other.

In this chapter we will look at the ethical principles behind some of the key environmental and social issues.

The focus of this book is on our interactions with the environment and the world at large, rather than on interpersonal behaviour – on how we behave as consumers (and disposers!). For the ethical consumer, this could translate to supporting the local organic farmer, and not buying clothes produced in Burmese sweatshops. On a global level, the ethical person would want to promote international peace, justice and fair trade, and would accept a responsibility to care for the environment. For the ethical consumer this could translate to boycotting companies and countries that abuse human rights, supporting fair trade initiatives and minimizing use of non-renewable resources.

The obvious catch is that it is not always clear – and it is often very difficult to find out – how, with what, and by whom goods have been produced. Being a truly ethical consumer requires a lot of knowledge, regular research and careful thought before every new purchase, and it will have a major impact on your own lifestyle. This book will point you along the road to being a truly ethical consumer, but it will also offer stopping points along the way. If all of us, to a greater or lesser extent, apply an awareness of the ethical and environmental issues to our consumption, then we can help to make the world a better place – for ourselves and for our grandchildren.

Making ethical choices

When you start to apply ethical principles to consumption decisions, you will see that they fall into five broad categories – with a lot of crossing over the boundaries between them:

* **The no-brainer.** Here the ethical issues are clear-cut, and the choice incurs no significant cost and requires no special effort, apart from thinking.
* **The must-do.** With this type of decision, the ethical issues are clear-cut, and should override any considerations of costs, effort, etc. For example, we should not be investing in, buying goods from or going as tourists to states like Burma where a military dictatorship kills and jails its pro-democracy opponents.

* **The worth doing.** This is really a subset of the must-do, and applies where ethical issues should be enough to outweigh considerations of slight extra cost, effort or discomfort. Fair trade foods do give Third World growers a better deal than they get from mainstream wholesalers, but they often cost a little more than normal.
* **The calculation.** There are energy/resources decisions which depend upon a number of factors that have to be balanced against one another. For example, the most eco-friendly car may not be the one that uses least petrol per mile, if you look at the total energy and resource usage over its lifetime. One of the big problems with this type of decision is that some of the figures may not be knowable, and others will be no more than best estimates.
* **The value-judgement.** There are situations where ethical issues overlap, and it is for each individual to decide which should prevail and to what extent. Where, for example, do you stand in the balance of animal rights against human safety? Would you refuse a life-saving drug because it had been tested on animals? How about a routine painkiller, a beauty product, a household cleaner?

Fortunately a lot of decisions fall into the first three categories, and calculations will only normally be needed once a year or so when a larger, long-life purchase is to be made.

Ethical companies

Sometimes what you are buying is less of an issue than who you are buying it from. Read the business pages, and you might be inclined to think that 'ethical company' is an oxymoron – there are certainly some who act as if the pursuit of profit can justify anything.

* **Nobody's perfect.** Some commercial activities are innately unethical. The oil business is the prime example. If a company is in the business of extracting, refining or selling oil, then it is actively contributing to global warming,

pollution and the depletion of the earth's scarce resources. The better companies in this field will be working harder to develop alternative energy supplies, to reduce spillages and waste, to encourage careful use, etc.

* **It's the company they keep.** Some firms don't seem to mind who they deal with. Those that trade in conflict diamonds bought from West African war lords are the extreme example, but far more common are those that source their toys or clothes from the cheapest possible manufacturer, no matter how low their workers' wages.
* **Corporate greed.** Large corporations make enormous profits and these may be fair profits for goods and services supplied. But some have no hesitation in taking the customers for all they can. Some exploit their own workers instead of or as well as their customers, siphoning off the profits into directors' pay and perks.
* **Fair deals.** There are some good companies out there, ones that strive to give a fair deal to their suppliers, workers and customers, and deal in eco-friendly products. Many of these are small, specialist firms, but there are bigger ones – the Co-op and the John Lewis partnership spring to mind.

Environmental issues

The ethical arguments here are essentially about 'stewardship'. There is nothing unethical, per se, in using energy and other resources. The problem lies in using up finite resources. We have a duty to future generations – our children and grandchildren, and their children and grandchildren. The earth's resources are finite and too many are being used up at an alarming rate. In the last 100 years, we have used the greater part of the world's known supplies of oil, copper, tin, silver and other key materials, and we are not likely to find large new stores of any of them. We are chopping down the world's great forests, emptying the once-teeming oceans of their fishes and whales, and burning so much coal and oil that we have changed the climate, making it hotter, wetter, wilder, more unpredictable and more damaging.

The rapid rise in CO_2 (carbon dioxide) levels is probably the most urgent problem we face. CO_2 is a part of the natural cycle, absorbed by plants where it is converted into starches, sugars and cellular material, and released through respiration, decay and natural forest and scrubland fires. It is also released – and in damaging quantities – by burning fossil fuels and clearing the great forests. In the 300 years since the start of the Industrial Revolution, concentrations of CO_2 have increased steadily, and have been rising at an exponential rate more recently. CO_2 is being produced at a rate faster than the natural world can absorb it, and levels are now higher than at any time in the last 160,000 years. CO_2 is a 'greenhouse gas', in that it tends to trap the sun's heat. To some extent this is a good thing – without the atmosphere's greenhouse effect we would all freeze to death in the winter (if not every night) – but the current high levels of CO_2 and other greenhouse gases are trapping too much and the earth is overheating.

Using renewable energy has no environmental impact in itself (though it does depend on what you use it for). The sun, wind, tides and rivers could provide all of the world's energy many times over – if these sources could be harnessed.

Food, wood, textile crops and other stuff we can grow are also renewable, but they can have environmental costs which we need to be aware of. Energy goes into their production, processing and distribution. Fertilizers and insecticides can poison the land and the rivers that they drain into. Sustainability is the key word here. Can we continue to replace what we take away in the long term? Can the energy costs be met from renewable sources?

Tipping the balance

There may be an argument for buying an 'energy-saving/-generating' device even though the actual lifetime energy costs/savings balance is negative. Sometimes you need to invest in a new technology to help to get it off the ground. The early models may take more energy to produce because they are not able to benefit from the economies of scale that come with a developed market; they may not deliver all that is hoped, partly because the technology is still in its infancy and partly because their working lives may well be relatively short. The petrol/electric hybrid cars are a good example of this. The models currently on sale are far from being the most energy-efficient cars on the market. More energy and resources are needed for their manufacture and maintenance – for a start, they need two engines (petrol and electric), and many of their components are so complex that they must be replaced, rather than repaired. As for fuel efficiency, there are plenty of cars with better miles per gallon figures – though most of them are smaller. But enough people are buying them to encourage manufacturers to continue developing the next generation of hybrids. (The other very positive aspect of these is that at least some of their buyers are choosing them because they are fashionable. And many of these would otherwise have bought 'Chelsea tractors'.)

Lifetime energy costs and savings

When you start looking at energy-saving devices, or at energy-generating devices, one of the things you must look at is their lifetime energy costs. These must then be balanced against the energy that they will save, or generate, during their working life. It's an exercise well worth doing, because what may seem a good ethical choice may not actually be so.

Domestic wind turbines are a good example of this. In theory, a small turbine can generate more energy than went into its manufacture in under a year, and it will go on generating surplus energy for at least another 30 years. In practice, if you install the turbine on a tower in an open site, exposed to the winds, it will perform to expectations, paying back its energy in the first year. Mount it on the roof of a house in the middle of town, and you will be lucky to generate enough energy to run a single light bulb – the total it produces during its working life will pay back no more than a fraction of its manufacturing energy costs. In the wrong place, a domestic wind turbine is an energy sink, so installing one would be a waste of resources.

Embodied energy and embodied carbon

'Embodied energy' refers to the energy that goes into the manufacture of an object; 'embodied carbon' is the CO_2 that was produced during its manufacture. The key problem in assessing these lies in knowing where to draw the line. It's not enough to simply take the total energy used by a factory and divide it by the number of objects produced. You also need to include the energy and CO_2 that went into the manufacture or extraction of the object's components or raw materials, plus that used in its transport, packaging, storage, marketing, and any other processes it goes through.

By themselves, embodied energy and carbon figures are not very meaningful, but where a set of similar objects has been assessed in the same way, the figures do show which is relatively more eco-friendly.

How do you measure up?

Before you go any further, take a few minutes to find out how far you are part of the problem, and how much you need to change if you are to live a sustainable, ethical lifestyle.

Ecological footprint

This is a way to measure your impact on the environment. It calculates how much of the earth's surface is needed to provide the energy, water and other resources that are needed to support your lifestyle, and also how much is required to absorb our carbon emissions and other waste. There are more and less complicated systems for calculating it – and none can ever be entirely accurate – but they do give you a point of comparison. You can compare your lifestyle with that of other people, and perhaps more valuably you can compare your lifestyle now with how it could be if you consumed more ethically.

The average European has a footprint of 6.3 hectares. If everyone on the planet lived at that level, we'd need 3.4 planets. It could be worse – the average US citizen has a footprint twice as large, so we'd need 6.6 planets for everyone to live the American life. What's your footprint? Best Foot Forward, ecological footprint experts, have a simple calculator on their website at: www.bestfootforward.com/footprintlife.htm.

Carbon footprint

This is a subset of the ecological footprint, but with the focus on global warming. It measures the carbon dioxide emissions for which you are responsible, directly through the use of fossil fuels for transport or in the home, and indirectly through your use of services and purchases of goods. The scientific consensus is that to stop global warming we all need to get our CO_2 emissions down to around 2,500 kg per year. Currently, the average in the UK is over 10,000 kg per year, so there's a lot of leeway to make up.

If you want to know your carbon footprint, and what you can do to reduce it, point your browser to: www.carbonfootprint.com.

The cost of ethical living

It's an obvious point, but one worth remembering – the poor take less from the world. People in Third World countries have far lower carbon footprints than we do in the West – the US produces over 20 tonnes of CO_2 per capita while, at the other end of the scale, in Chad the emission rate is 0.1 tonnes. And in the West, those who cannot afford a car or foreign holidays have lower footprints than the rich. It's not surprising then that many of the things you can do to lower your footprint will save you money. Most will cost you nothing more than a little thought and effort; some will involve making changes to your lifestyle.

Reducing your environmental impact is a major part of ethical living, and something that can be done at no financial cost.

Support for human rights and for fair trade does have cost implications – sometimes you have to reach deeper into your pocket to do the right thing.

The good neighbour

In this book, the focus is on the practical aspects of ethical living, but the human aspects should not be neglected. Researchers consistently find that the happiest societies are not the wealthiest ones, but those where there is the strongest sense of community – where people care for others beyond their immediate family and friends. Being a good neighbour is important. We should all be ready to lend each other a hand in times of need, to share in taking care of the area, to look out for the very old and the very young, and to give some of our time and energy to the community. Who are our neighbours? What is our community? Well, we all live in a global village now so we need to look far outwards, but your community starts in the streets around your house.

2

energy

We use energy, of one sort or another, in everything we do. In this chapter, we're looking at energy in the home – how much we use, how we use it, and how we can use less of it. And we do need to use less of it. The problem is not that using energy is of itself a bad thing – it isn't. The problem is where that energy comes from, and currently virtually all of the energy we use comes from coal, oil and gas. These are non-renewable, and running out, and their combustion in engines, turbines, boilers and for space heating is a major cause of climate change. Until we can get all our energy from renewable, non-polluting sources, we are going to have to use it a lot more carefully.

Energy sources

First of all, where does the energy come from? The best and latest estimates show that in 2007, the UK consumed oil, gas, coal, nuclear electricity and renewable energy totalling the equivalent of nearly 230 million tonnes of oil.

Oil is by far the most important source of energy for us at the moment, and we must reduce our consumption for two main reasons:

* It's running out. We have already taken more out of our own North Sea fields than is left in them, and in the world as a whole we are currently either at or just past peak production. From now onwards, oil will be increasingly scarce.
* Burning oil, in vehicle engines or in boilers, produces CO_2 – the main greenhouse gas, and a major factor in climate change.

Gas is mainly used for generating electricity, for space heating and in industry. Like oil, this is a limited resource and its use helps to drive climate change. We have pretty much burnt our way through the gas from the North Sea fields – they will be exhausted within the next 20 years – and we are becoming dependent on imports from Russia and elsewhere.

Coal is almost entirely used for generating electricity. It is a finite resource – they stopped making coal in the Jurassic era – though the world's reserves should last for another couple of hundred years. The crunch point here is that, even with the latest, cleanest technology, coal still produces greenhouse gases when burnt. And if you don't use the latest, cleanest technology, it produces noxious smoke laden with lung-damaging particles, sulphur, and a range of other pollutants.

Electricity in this context refers only to that produced by nuclear power. Currently around 15 per cent of our total electricity is nuclear, but this is declining as old stations reach the end of their safe operational life.

Renewables include wind, solar, hydro, tidal, wood, biomass and other sources of energy that are replenished by nature.

Capturing and using the sun's energy, whether as electricity from a solar cell or as wood from a tree, does not add to the greenhouse effect. Instead you become part of the natural cycle. If all our energy came from renewable sources, energy use would not be an issue. But they don't, and so it is.

No-brainer

If you have not already done so, switch to a green energy supplier now. It's actually very little trouble (normally). Five minutes online will establish the best green supplier for you – their charges vary according to where you are, though their CO_2 emissions/kWh are the same. Despite expectations, green energy can be cheaper than energy from standard sources. Green electricity is conceivable – it can be generated from hydro-electric schemes, wind farms and other renewables – but is there really such a thing as green gas? Yes, because the gas suppliers offset their carbon emissions, generally by investing in renewable electricity projects.

The green helpline (www.greenhelpline.com) is just one of several sites where you can compare gas and electric prices, and then arrange to change your supplier. Other switching sites include uSwitch (www.uSwitch.com/energy/green-energy.html) and Consumer Direct (www.consumerdirect.gov.uk) who also carry good information about just how green these 'green' energy suppliers are.

Energy use in the home

About 30 per cent of the national energy total is used in the home (equivalent to 47 million tonnes of oil) – more than in industry, though less than in transport. The proportion and the total amount have both been rising steadily over the years, though not, thankfully, as fast as they might. The Office of National Statistics estimates that without the insulation and energy-saving measures that are already in place, we would be using energy at almost twice the current level.

At present, less than 1 per cent of this energy comes from renewable resources. Of the rest, 70 per cent is gas, 21 per cent electric (mostly produced from coal and gas) and 7 per cent oil. Their use is a major part of the UK's CO_2 emissions. We must reduce our use of those finite resources, and we can. But how?

Space heating

Space heating accounts for about 60 per cent of the energy used in homes. And a lot of that is wasted. Let's see what we can do.

No-brainer

With some things, the saving of energy – and money – is so obvious, there really is no excuse for not doing them. They take nothing more than a little thought and effort:

* Turning the thermostat down by 1°C could reduce your heating bill by up to 10 per cent, saving around £25 a year, and you probably would not notice the difference.
* Only heat the house when it is needed. Set the timer to come on half an hour before you get up in the morning and before you come home in the evening. Set it to go off half an hour before you go to work, or before you go to bed at night.
* If a room is not normally used, turn its radiator off and close the door.
* Close the curtains on cold evenings. If the sun's not coming in through the windows, heat is going out.

Must-do

* An un-insulated house wastes a tremendous amount of energy. Insulation costs money, but most forms will repay the investment in as little as two years by dramatically reducing your energy use/heating bills – and the house will be more comfortable to live in now that it no longer has cold spots and damp walls. In a typical

un-insulated semi-detached house, around one-third of the heat is lost through the walls, one-third through the roof, 20 per cent through draughts and poor ventilation, and the rest through the windows.

* The loft should have at least 25 cm of insulation. If there is nothing there already, this is the most effective step you can take, giving the quickest payback at low cost.
* Cavity wall insulation is the next best step. This will typically repay its cash investment (and energy cost) in around two years.

Worth doing

There are more energy savings to be made. These will take a bit more effort, or longer to recoup their costs, but are still well worth doing:

* Not all rooms need to be the same temperature – the recommended levels are 21°C (70°F) in the living, dining and bathroom, and 18°C (65°F) elsewhere. Room thermostats allow you to control the temperature of each room individually. They will cost around £15 each, plus fitting, but should recoup their cost in a couple of years.
* Draught proofing windows and doors is inexpensive. The savings are not great, but it will make rooms more comfortable. Just don't overdo it! You need some air circulation, especially if there is a gas fire in the room.

Calculate the cost

On the heating and insulation front there are two areas where you may need to think carefully before you make changes: the boiler and the windows. If you are building a new house, or replacing a worn-out boiler or a rotted window frame, there is no problem – you go for the most energy-efficient solution. But if you are thinking about replacing something which still has a useful life, this has environmental implications. You have to balance the carbon and energy costs of manufacturing the new equipment, and of disposing of the old ones, against the savings once they are installed.

Gas boilers

Since 2005, you have only been allowed to install a boiler with an efficiency rating of A or B and that basically means a condensing boiler. These condense the exhaust gases, capturing much of the heat that would otherwise go up the flue, and pass it back into the water heating system. In theory, a condensing boiler can achieve 90 per cent efficiency, but that is only under optimal conditions, with the equipment operating at its peak. These boilers are more complex than the traditional alternative, have more to go wrong and need more frequent servicing to keep at their best, so, in practice, you should assume an efficiency closer to 80 per cent. That is about 10 to 15 per cent better than a properly maintained traditional boiler.

Condensing boilers are relatively new technology, and so far we have only estimates of their lifespan, but their extra complexity makes it likely that they won't last the 25 years that you would expect from a traditional one. This hits the cost-balance. A new boiler will cost between £1,500 and £2,250 to install. If you have already done the 'no-brainer', 'must-do' and 'worth doing' energy-saving steps then your current heating bills will have already been reduced – perhaps down to £500 or £600 p.a. on a family home. On current energy prices, a 15 per cent increase in efficiency would deliver savings of under £100 and would take 15 to 25 years to recoup the investment. Energy prices are highly likely to continue to rise, so the effective payback time could be within the life of the boiler. The energy payback time – that saved by its use compared with the energy used in its manufacture – should be considerably shorter.

Alternative 1: Wood stoves and boilers

Wood is a carbon-neutral fuel, in that it absorbs as much CO_2 while it's growing as it releases when it's burnt. And if the wood comes from a managed source, then the cycle continues.

If you want to run central heating from wood, you can use a stove with a back boiler, but you are probably better off with a boiler, and preferably one that runs on wood chips or pellets (processed waste from sawmills). These can be set to run automatically, with the fuel stored in a hopper and fed in on demand.

Wood is a cheaper fuel than either gas or electricity – about 25 per cent cheaper when used as a room heater, and up to 50 per cent in a central heating system.

Alternative 2: Heat pumps

Heat pumps are refrigerators in reverse – at least, they are the reverse in their effect, but the technology is identical. A heat pump draws low grade heat from one source and transfers it, as higher grade heat, to another. In a fridge, it takes heat from inside and radiates it out the back; in a domestic heat pump, it takes heat from outside and brings it into the house. It's all based on the thermal qualities of gas – if you compress gas, it gets hotter and will radiate out the heat; if you expand it, it gets cooler and will absorb any heat from its surroundings. It is a highly efficient system, producing 3 to 4 kilowatts of heat for every 1 kWh used to power the pump.

Domestic heat pump systems are usually geothermal – they draw their heat from the ground. In the UK, the ground rarely freezes more than a spade's depth down, and once you get below about 1 metre, its temperature is pretty constant, and can typically range from 7°C to 13°C. This is a viable heat source, especially as the ground has such thermal mass that you can draw from it steadily throughout the colder months without significantly lowering its temperature. The heat-collector is normally a continuous run of flexible piping, laid horizontally about 1 metre below the surface. If you do not have sufficient area available, the pipework can be installed vertically – which needs more specialized equipment. The heat pump itself is the size of a large boiler. It can be fitted to an exterior wall, or tucked into the garage.

Heat pumps are best used with underfloor heating. They can be used with radiators, but because they don't get the water as hot as a boiler will, you need more or bigger radiators to heat the same space.

Once installed, the system should need minimal maintenance – when did you last have to do anything to your fridge, apart from clearing out uneaten food? The pipework should be good for at least 50 years, and heat pumps have a life expectancy of 25+ years.

The savings are good. You will be using up to 75 per cent less energy to heat your home, and with electricity from a green supplier, that will mean zero CO_2 emissions. You should save £400 to £600 a year in energy bills.

To get a better idea of prices and designs, visit one or more of these sites: Ice Energy (www.iceenergy.co.uk), Earth Energy (www.earthenergy.co.uk) or Eco heat pumps (www.ecoheatpumps.co.uk).

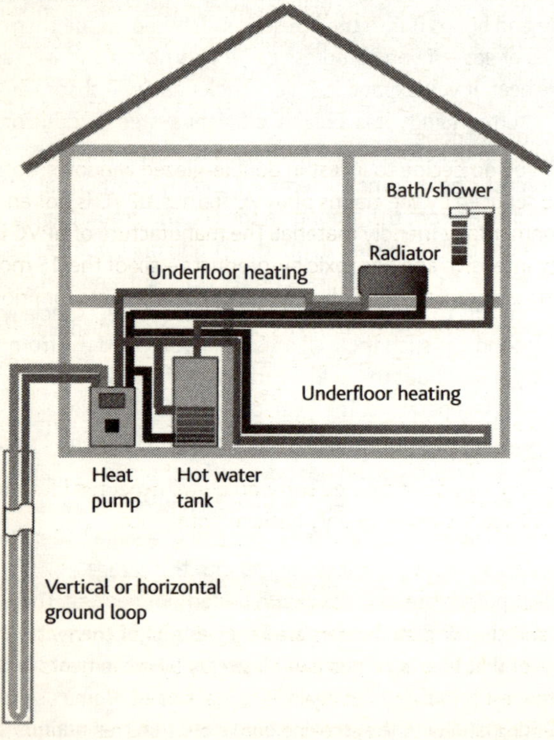

Figure 2.1 *The ground beneath our houses is a reliable – and renewable – source of heat.*

Double glazing

Single-glazed windows radiate heat to the great outdoors. Double-glazed windows also radiate heat, though at only half the rate.

Windows also let in light and heat. The heat gain through a south-facing double-glazed window over the winter months can be equal to the heat loss, so their effective U value is zero.

In terms of energy saving, you certainly need some form of secondary glazing, but proper double glazing is expensive. For a family home, the saving will only be around £100 a year, but the cost is likely to be between £3,000 and £4,000. Even with rising energy prices, you probably will not recoup the investment within the lifetime of the windows (of which more shortly). Secondary internal glazing, using acrylic sheet, or glass, in plastic or metal frames, should cost under £500 as a DIY job, or around £1,000 professionally done.

If you do decide to invest in double-glazed windows, do not be seduced by the claims of uPVC frames. uPVC is not an environmentally friendly material. The manufacture of uPVC is energy intensive and has toxic by-products – six of the 15 most hazardous chemicals listed by European governments for priority elimination are released during its production and disposal. Though they are advertised as maintenance-free, in practice the frames only have a lifespan of 20 to 25 years before they begin to go brittle. And once they do start to go, they cannot be repaired, but must be replaced completely.

Frames made of treated softwood have expected lifetimes of 25 to 30 years, even with only basic maintenance.

Patio heaters

Gas and electric patio heaters are very wasteful of energy. Much of that heat is carried away instantly by movements of the air; the rest is radiated out again as it is absorbed. Home use is increasing, and with the smoking ban in pubs and restaurants, which came into force in 2007, we now face an explosion in their use.

One patio heater running all evening (and some lunchtimes), through much of the year can produce almost 4 tonnes of CO_2 a year: that's around two-thirds of an average household's total emissions. If you are cold when sitting outside, put a jumper on. If some form of heating is necessary, buy a wood-burning chimenea.

Water heating

On average 23 per cent of domestic energy is used for heating water. How much of that is necessary?

No-brainer

There's no point in heating more water than we need, or to a higher temperature than is needed:

* Set your tank thermostat to 60°C, which is more than hot enough for any domestic purposes. You could drop it a couple of degrees below this, but it must not be run below 55°C, because bacteria, such as those that cause Legionnaires disease, can survive up to there.
* Set the timer so that the water heats up for when you need it, but is off for the rest of the day. With a well-insulated tank, there is very little heat loss.
* A shower typically uses less than half as much hot (and cold) water as a bath, though power showers use about the same amount.
* Don't wash yourself – or anything else – under a running hot tap.

Must-do

Few houses nowadays have un-insulated hot water tanks – for some years now, most have been pre-fitted with a solid foam jacket. If you have a loose jacket, check its depth – it should be at least 10 cm. Replacing a thin or badly fitting jacket will cost around £15 and pay for itself in two years.

Worth doing

Solar water heating is a viable option that we should all be considering. The technology is now well developed, and the benefits proven. It can deliver up to 90 per cent of a house's hot water in the summer, and capture some heat even in the winter. Overall, you can expect to reduce your water heating bills by around 70 per cent in the UK. A two-panel system, suitable for a family of four, will cost a little over £3,000 to install and should save about £80 p.a. A solar system will recover its embodied energy in three to five years, and its embodied carbon in seven to ten years. At current prices, it would take over 30 years to recoup the investment, but as energy prices are likely to rise, the actual payback time will probably be much less.

Lighting

The electricity used in lights and appliances adds up to around 12 per cent of the total energy used in a home. Few of these use much energy individually, so the potential savings on any given usage is quite small, but this is a case of 'many a mickel makes a muckel'. For example, if every household in the country replaced five standard 100 watt bulbs with the equivalent energy-efficient 20 watt bulbs, the combined saving would be over 5,000 Megawatts and we could shut Drax, the largest coal-fired power station in the UK. This would reduce our CO_2 emissions by over 20 million tonnes! Every little helps!

No-brainer

* Walk round the house. Take a note of every light and appliance, and ask yourself, 'Does this need to be on?' If not, turn it off.
* Get into the habit of turning lights off as you leave the room.
* Turn off the TV, radio and computer when you have finished using them – and turn them off completely, rather than leaving them on standby. It's estimated that in the UK the total energy consumed by appliances on standby is responsible for one million tonnes of CO_2 emissions.

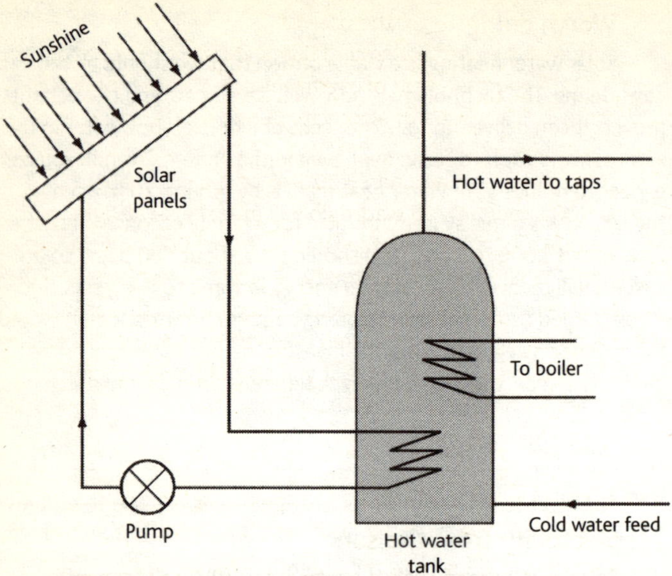

Figure 2.2 *A basic solar system. A fluid is pumped through the collector panels, then through a coil in the hot water tank. The tank also has a second coil, heated by a standard boiler, to be used as necessary.*

Must-do

In a standard tungsten light bulb, the majority of the energy is transformed into heat, and less than 20 per cent into visible light. Fluorescent tubes are far more efficient, converting virtually all of the energy into light – but, until recently, it wasn't the sort of light that people wanted in the living areas of their homes. The cold, faintly blue light was acceptable in offices and shops, and even in utility rooms, kitchens and bathrooms, but not elsewhere. Their long thin shapes also limited the places in which they could be used.

Things have changed. The new generation of CFL bulbs produce a quality of light that is at least as warm and natural as that from a tungsten bulb, and they are available as twisted tubes, or enclosed bulbs the same shape as tungsten ones.

The numbers speak for themselves:

* Tungsten bulbs cost around 30p and have a life of about 1,000 hours – a year of average use. A 100 watt bulb will use 100 kilowatts of electricity during its life, at a cost of just over £7.
* CFL bulbs cost around £3.50 and have a life of about 8,000 hours. An 18 watt bulb will give the same light output as a 100 watt tungsten bulb. In 1,000 hours it will use 18 kilowatts of electricity, at a cost of just over £1.20.

Long before you have reached the end of the first year, the energy saving will have covered the extra cost of the CFL bulb. Over the lifetime of the CFL bulb, it will use £10 of electricity, while its eight tungsten equivalents will use £56.

Invest in the future

Electricity from the sun

Solar cells, properly called photovoltaic (PV) cells generate electricity from sunlight – and though they work best in full sunlight, they can still generate in cloudy weather, as long as there is some daylight. They are unobtrusive and silent in operation. Once installed, they should require no maintenance for the rest of their 30+ years' life, and over that time a typical domestic PV system could save over 30 tonnes of CO_2 emissions.

Practical matters

The thing about solar cells is that they generate electricity most when you need them least – unless you work from home and use electrical equipment, or watch a lot of daytime TV. The other notable thing about them is that they produce DC (direct current) electricity – what you get from batteries, rather than AC (alternating current) that you get from the mains. The net result is that what you get out of PV cells is not exactly what you need.

If you attach an inverter to the cells, this will convert the DC to AC power, and you can feed the output directly into the mains. This is the simple solution, but inverters do add to the cost of the system and reduce the output slightly – there is some loss of power during conversion.

There are several solutions to the time-based production/need dilemma. The most common is to connect your installation to the national grid. When you are generating more than you are using, the excess flows into the grid – in effect, winding your metre backwards – and when you are not generating enough for your needs, you draw it from the grid as usual.

Mounting options

On an existing house, the best solution is normally a set of panels, mounted above the roof. Ideally, it should face due south, but it could be as far round as south east or south west without reducing the output by more than a few per cent.

PV cells can also be fitted in place of normal roof tiles. The units are typically the width of four tiles, and the depth of one or two, and can be fitted to the standard battens.

There are also façade materials, with built-in thin-film PV cells, which can be used for external wall cladding. Their striking appearance makes these more suitable for office blocks than for domestic buildings.

Outputs and costs

The output from a PV system is rated in Wp (peak Wattage) – its maximum. As the maximum is only reached in ideal conditions, and only for part of each day even then, the more useful measure is kWh p.a. (kilowatt hours per year). A typical two-panel 100 Wp installation on a well-lit site will generate around 1,500 kWh per year. That's about 5 kWh per day, or an average of 1 kWh an hour during the evenings. You could generate enough to run your (low-energy) lights and a TV or PC. At current prices, the value is a little over £150 per year. As such systems cost over £12,000, the financial return does not look good – a little over 1 per cent – but that's not the whole story. There are government grants available for householders, and these can cover up to 50 per cent of the cost. The grants are, at present, in short supply – you have to work at it, and be lucky, to get one. Secondly, electricity prices will almost certainly rise in the future. With a grant

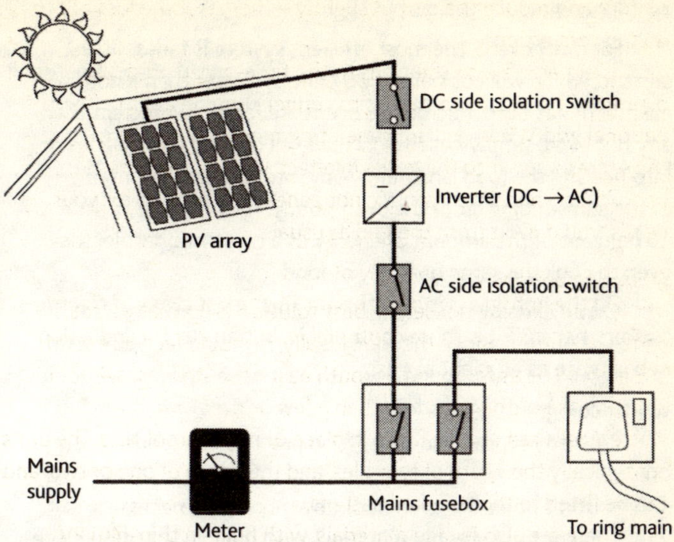

Figure 2.3 *The elements of a typical roof-mounted PV system, linked to the mains supply.*

and higher prices, a PV installation is probably a good long-term investment even in purely financial terms. In energy terms, it is certainly a good investment as long as you have a suitable site.

Solar electricity systems will get cheaper and more efficient. Once the thin-film PV technology reaches the mass production stage, we should see a distinct drop in the cost of systems, and an improvement in their efficiency.

Cooking

On average, cooking takes around 3 per cent of the energy used in our homes. That doesn't leave a lot of room for major savings, but the kitchen should not be ignored.

When you are measuring the efficiency of a cooking method, what you are looking at is the transfer of heat to food – which may sound a bit obvious, but there is a point to this.

Cookers

For (hot) ovens, the most efficient system is fan-assisted electric, which will cook about 20 per cent faster than a normal electric or gas oven. Microwave ovens are far more efficient than any hot oven, simply because virtually all of their energy goes into heating the food, and hardly any into the food's container or the surrounding air or the oven's body. They can use as little as 10 per cent of the amount of energy as a conventional electric oven to cook the same quantity of food.

On the hob, gas is more efficient than most types of electric cookers, because it is more controllable, but an electric induction hob is twice as efficient as gas.

Worth doing

With any types of cookers, good practice can reduce energy use:

* Don't open the oven door any more than necessary. Every time you open it, you lower the inside temperature and increase the cooking time.
* Turn off electric ovens several minutes before the end of the cooking time. It will stay hot enough to finish cooking, as long as the door stays closed.
* On the hob, use pans the same size as the ring, as far as possible. With a small pan on a large ring, much heat is lost up the sides.
* Put lids on pans unless there is a reason not to. Water will come to the boil faster, and will need less heat to keep boiling with the lid on.

Kettles

The key here is not to boil any more water than you need at the time. There are two sides to this:

* You need a kettle that can boil a small amount – and that means either an old-fashioned metal one that goes on the hob, or an electric one with the element below the base plate.

* You have to get into the habit of only putting in what you need. Most of the electric 'jug' kettles have measuring scales on a clear window or on the inside.

If you live in a hard water area, you need to keep limescale under control. Scale on the element or base plate will reduce efficiency. To remove it, put enough vinegar into the kettle to cover the limescale and leave overnight, then rinse out in the morning.

Electrical appliances

There are two aspects to and two questions about energy use with any electrical appliance. The first, and most obvious, is the energy needed to run it, and how you can minimize that. The second is the energy that went into its manufacture, and how you can get maximum value out of that. The first aspect is the easiest to tackle – it's simple to find out how much energy an appliance uses when it is running, and simple to control how much it runs. We'll look at this more closely as we work through different types of appliances.

The second aspect is much more difficult – there are no reliable, comparable published figures that will tell you how much energy goes into making appliances. However, there are some handy rules of thumb for maximizing the use of this energy, and they apply to all types of equipment:

* Use it until it dies. The only exception to this is where you have a very inefficient old appliance and can replace it with one which will do the same job using, say, half the energy.
* Simpler is better. Every extra function, gadget or option built into an appliance took energy to develop and manufacture and is another thing to go wrong, potentially reducing its lifespan (see point 1).
* Beware cheap and cheerful. If it's cheaper because it's simpler (see point 2), that's good; if it's cheaper because it's less well-made, that's bad. If you pay 20 per cent more but get an appliance which will last 50 per cent longer – well, you do the maths.

EU Energy labels

By law, the European Community Energy Label must be displayed on all new household electrical products.

The labels all have the key energy rating at the top, but then vary according to the type of appliance. If it meets other environmental criteria, the appliance may have been awarded the Ecolabel Flower.

Washing machines

Heating the water is what takes the energy in a washing machine – agitating and spinning the drum take relatively little. The 95°C setting should never be needed – the clothes will come out as clean from a 60°C wash, and the machine will use half the electricity. Most of the time, a 30°C wash will do the job perfectly well, though you may need to switch to a washing powder that is designed for lower temperatures.

Buying guide

When choosing a new washing machine, check the energy labels. You want one that has an A-rating for energy efficiency and which uses the least amount of water, proportionate to the load size. The difference between the most and the least efficient is quite marked – from 1.2 kWh to 2 kWh for the same washing cycle. A 30° option is essential.

Tumble dryers

The sun and wind do a better job for drying clothes – and that's all totally renewable energy! But if you have no garden, this is not an option. Gas-heated tumble dryers are more energy efficient, though more expensive.

Dishwashers

Let's start with some good news: if you have a lot of washing up to do, it is more energy efficient to do it in the dishwasher than by hand. Why? Because the dishwasher will use considerably less hot water to get the same results.

Two tips for optimum energy efficiency:

* Wait until you have a full load – if there is going to be a long delay before the other half of the load will appear, run a short rinse cycle so that food doesn't dry hard onto the plates.
* It takes more energy to dry dishes than to wash them, so let them dry naturally. If your machine does not have no-dry option, stop the cycle after the last draining and open the door to let the dishes air dry.

Buying guide

Dishwashers fall into two main categories – undercounter and slimline. Undercounter models typically have space for 12 settings, and have fairly similar performance in terms of energy use. Slimline models typically take eight settings, but show more variation in their efficiency.

Buy one to suit your family size and eating habits. If you aren't using it at least four or five times a week, it's too big.

Check the energy label – nowadays they are pretty well all A-rated for energy efficiency, but there's some variation in their washing and drying efficiencies.

Fridges and freezers

Fridges and freezers are essentially insulated boxes that work best when full and unopened. The problem is that air moves of its own accord. Open the door and half a fridgeful of cold air falls onto the floor and is replaced with warm air from the room. If the fridge is largely empty, then a lot of cold escapes whenever the door is opened. For every minute that the door is open, it can take three to five minutes' running to restore the internal temperature.

Upright freezers suffer from the same problem. Internal doors to the shelves, or drawers instead of shelves can help to reduce cold loss. Chest freezers are better in this respect, as the heavy, cold air will stay in place when the lid is lifted, though some will be displaced while you are digging down to the bottom for that emergency loaf you know is down there somewhere.

Worth doing

* If you have a separate freezer, does it need to be in the kitchen? Where is the coolest place in your house or garage?
* Make sure that there is enough space behind and above the fridge and freezer for circulation of air to carry away heat from the grill.
* Keep the appliance full to reduce cold air loss when the door is opened. Crumpled newspaper is an effective space filler.
* Get a fridge thermometer and check the temperatures. (Fridges should run at 0–4°C and freezers at –18°C).
* Defrost the freezer regularly, for greatest efficiency.

Buying guide

* Don't buy anything bigger than you need. If the fridge or freezer is not going to be at least two-thirds full most of the time, then you will not be using it efficiently.
* Check the EU energy label. The best have A+ or even A++ energy efficiency ratings.

A smaller appliance will not necessarily use less energy. The least energy-efficient fridge-freezer on the market at the time of writing was an LG with a fridge capacity of 3.9 cubic feet and a 2.2 cubic feet freezer, but consumes a whopping 474 kWh per year. Compare this with the current best, the Siemens KG 36 × 47 with a 7.9 cubic feet fridge and a 3.2 cubic feet freezer that uses only 208 kWh per year (figures from www.sust-it.net).

Electronic equipment

The main issue with electronic equipment is about unnecessary use of energy. DVD players, Freeview boxes and other entertainment equipment often do not have off switches, but go into standby mode when not in use, so that they can be fired up again by the remote. In some cases, if you do turn them off at the wall socket, then you may lose current data, e.g. where you had got to in the DVD when you stopped watching. Normally the only effect of turning them off at the mains is that you have to walk across the room to turn them back on again, instead of slumping straight onto the couch and reaching for the remote.

It's worth comparing the total usage when active and when on standby. Take DVD players for example. A reasonably efficient player runs at around 10 watts when active, and 1 watt on standby. As the player will typically be active for perhaps two hours a day, and on standby for 22, you get the following consumption patterns:

Active	10 w × 2 hours =	20 w/hr
Standby	1 w × 22 hours =	22 w/hr
Daily total		42 w/hr

This is using more power when not in use than when it is!

With electronic equipment, one of the interesting things is how much variation there is in their efficiency. You might think, for instance, that a 32-inch TV would use much the same amount of energy, whoever makes it. There is a huge difference between the best and the worst, at least among those with LCD screens – the most efficient, the Loewe Xelos, uses only 75 watts an hour compared with the Samsung equivalent which uses 275 watts – over three times as much. There is rather less variation with the cathode ray tube sets. The best of these, from Philips, uses 109 watts an hour, while the least efficient, from Beko, burns only 50 per cent more at 165 watts.

No-brainer

* Turn equipment off at the mains after use. When buying new, look for models that have an off switch on the box.
* Check out the energy use of any equipment before buying, and aim for the most efficient. You can find the figures for most types and models at Sust-it (www.sust-it.net).

Computers ...

The energy demands of PCs varies considerably. The greenest is the Tranquil PC, which consumes under 30 watts (standby 2 watts); the worst currently is the Dell Dimension 9200 which uses 257 watts when fully active, 211 watts in its so-called 'idle' mode, but only 2.2 watts on standby. And this is just the box. Monitors use anything from 20 to 60 watts (17-inch LCD).

Worth doing

* Do a full shut down and turn off the power unless you are coming back to the PC shortly.
* When buying a new PC, make power consumption one of the key considerations – check them out at www.sust-it.net.

... and printers

The main issue with printers is not the energy they use – which is not much – but the resources that go into ink and toner cartridges. It takes over a litre of oil to manufacture a laser printer cartridge, and around half that to make an ink jet cartridge. Though almost all are refillable, most are used only once before they head for landfill. The UK has one of the worst recycling rates in Europe for cartridges, with perhaps 10,000 tonnes of them sent to landfill each year.

Printer manufacturers do not encourage refilling, simply because so much of their profit comes from the sale of cartridges. Some have even built chips into the cartridge to prevent them from being refilled – the chip must be reprogrammed or replaced, along with the toner.

No-brainer

Recycle your old cartridges. Remanufacturers will pay for them, giving the money either to you or to a charity. Many cartridges come with envelopes that you can use to post the cartridge to the remanufacturers – Tommy's, the baby charity, is very active in this area and makes over £50,000 a year through cartridge recycling.

Make money by recycling

If you have a steady stream of used cartridges to dispose of in your work, or you are looking for a new source of revenue for your school or club, there are businesses that will pay you directly for them. Values range from 5p to £2.50 each, depending upon their type and whether they have already been refilled, but if you have enough cartridges coming in, it may be worth the effort of organizing it. Two firms to talk to are Cartridge Express at www.cartridgeexpress.net and Cash for Cartridges at www.cashforcartridges.co.uk.

Worth doing

* Have your old cartridges refilled at Cartridge World. It will usually cost around half as much as a new one. This is a national franchised business – find your nearest branch at www.cartridgeworld.org.
* Try refilling your own laser printer cartridges. Toner Top-up sells bottles of toner, and refilling tools for DIY refilling. On average you can refill a cartridge three times before one of its moving components wears out. Find out more at www.tonertopup.co.uk.

How much electricity are you using?

And that's 'how much right now'? If you have an electricity usage monitor you can see exactly how much energy you are using, while you are using it. Why would you want to know? Mainly because it gets you to focus on the question of how much electricity you actually need to use. With a monitor in your hand, you will find yourself irresistibly drawn to walking round the house turning things on to see how much they use, then off – and leaving them off if possible. People who fit them typically find that they save the cost of the meter within months, and go on to have lower electricity bills – and carbon footprint – because they have got into the habit of turning things off.

There are several monitors on the market at present; two worth investigating are:

* Efergy home CO_2 meter from Sust-it at www.sust-it.net
* The Owl electricity monitor from Let's Automate at www.letsautomate.com.

They are both around £50 and very similar in design. Each has two components: a device which fits around the mains supply, measures the current flow and transmits that data; and a hand-held receiver which displays the flow in terms of electricity use, CO_2 emissions or money, so that you can see how much of any of them you are using/wasting. Fitting is simple – you just clip the sensor around the mains wire between the electricity meter and the fuse box, stick batteries into the hand-held unit and that's it. The only catch is that the sensor/transmitter unit needs power, so you'll need a socket within reach.

Disposal and recycling

All appliances reach the end of their useful life sometime. And then what? With white goods – fridges, cookers, washing machines and the like – there is usually a very simple answer. Most retailers now will remove an old machine when they deliver a new one, and they will send it on for recycling. If this is not an option, your local council-run recycling centre will take them, and if you cannot get them there yourself, councils normally offer a collection service for bulky goods. Recycling fridges and freezers actually costs money – recovering the refrigerant gases is a specialized job – but the sheet metal in white goods gives them some scrap value.

TVs, DVD players and other electronic goods tend to have shorter lives, and are rarely worth repairing nowadays – it's often cheaper to buy new than have equipment repaired. When you do replace appliances, ask the retailer if they will take the old one, and if not, drop it into the local recycling centre.

If an appliance – white goods or electronics – is still working, look for ways to extend its life. Is there a Freecycle group (see Chapter 3) in your area? Contact your local Social Services to see if they have any schemes for reusing working appliances.

3

in the home

In Chapter 2, we looked at the use of energy in the home, and that reducing must be the first priority in making our homes greener places, but there are other issues. We need to look at the chemicals that we use to freshen and clean our houses, and ourselves; at the resources that go into our furniture and decorations – and at how and where they are manufactured; and at our water use. As in other areas of our lives, being more environmentally friendly at home will typically save you money, though it may well require a little thought, and sometimes a little more effort. We'll start the greening of our homes with water use, because that's where there are some of the simpler decisions and easier savings to be made.

Water use

The issues with water are primarily about limited resources and energy use. Here in the UK we have more than enough rainfall in total to meet our current needs, but not necessarily in the right place or at the right time, and on past trends our needs will rise in the future. The rain falls mainly in the north west while the bulk of the population, and much of the industrial and agricultural demand, is located in the south east.

Even if there was an endless supply of water in the pipes, we should still minimize our usage because of the energy costs. It takes energy to filter, purify and pump water from rivers or underground sources to our homes, and to run the treatment plants to clean waste water before it is returned to the environment. Overall, the water industry uses 2 per cent of the total energy consumed in the UK, and is responsible for 1 per cent of the CO_2 emissions. When you waste water, you also waste energy, and add to greenhouse gases.

No-brainer

* Try not to let a tap run, unused, straight down the plughole.
* When you do have to run the tap to get hot water, you might collect that run-off for watering plants in the garden or on the patio.
* If you are a gardener, fit a water butt to a downpipe and collect rainwater. If your tap water is hard, some plants, especially heathers and azaleas, will appreciate the softness of rainwater.
* Showers normally use less water than baths, though the difference is less marked with power showers.
* Fix dripping taps. Installing a new washer is normally a simple DIY job.

Worth doing

* If you haven't already got one, have a water meter installed. There is nothing like knowing that you are paying by the litre to make you use less water.

* Install a low-flush or dual-flush toilet. Over 30 per cent of the water used in most homes goes straight down the loo. A low-flush toilet will reduce this to under 25 per cent.
* Taps with aerators use up to 50 per cent less water when things are being washed beneath a running tap. You may be able to fit aerators into existing taps.
* Fit a water-saving head into the shower.
* When watering patio plants or flower beds, a watering can may be more bother, but it puts water only where it is most needed, and you will use significantly less.

Cleaning

The issues here are about the impact of cleaning products on the environment and on our health. Is it sensible to spray toxic compounds onto our kitchen work surfaces, into our washing bowls, into the air and onto ourselves in the name of 'cleanliness'?

Fresh air

According to the US Environmental Protection Agency, the levels of pollutants (mainly VOCs) can be from 2 to 100 times higher inside a home than outdoors.

Air fresheners are a particular cause for concern. A study, published in *New Scientist* found that people who used air fresheners were 25 per cent more likely to suffer from headaches, and in 2007, the European Community Respiratory Health Survey showed that the use of cleaning sprays and air fresheners increased the risk of asthma by between 30 per cent and 50 per cent.

The petrochemicals and synthetic scents used in air fresheners cause considerable concern, but where the ingredients are purely natural, this does not necessarily make them safe. Terpenes are chemicals found in citrus oils. They are not harmful when released into the air, but they can react with ozone. In the home and offices, this is produced by printers and photocopiers. There are even special 'air purifiers' that generate ozone, which is supposed to improve air quality. Terpenes and ozone combine to form formaldehyde, a respiratory irritant and a known carcinogen.

No-brainer

* Open the windows and let some fresh air in to drive out the smells.
* Bring flowers in from the garden, or buy them and enjoy their scents.
* Keep house plants – broad-leaved ones are best. They help to filter the air.
* Baking soda will absorb odours from the air and also from carpets and furniture.

Household cleaners

Household cleaners can be very nasty products. There are some very potent chemicals out there on the shelves – especially in the products designed for the worst jobs. Around 2 per cent of hospital admissions are the direct result of exposure to household cleaners, and the long-term damage to health is something that we are only now starting to understand.

To be *absolutely* sure that the cleaners that you use, in the combinations that you use them, are *absolutely* safe for you, your family or the environment, you can either:

* get a degree in chemistry and another in toxicology, or
* use only the simplest, most basic products.

The former of these options may not be possible for most of us, but the latter *is*, and we will come back to it. If you don't need absolutes, then life is a little more manageable.

No-brainer

Choose eco-friendly products from environmentally aware firms. If you want to be sure that the product is truly eco-friendly, look for the EU Eco-label. Anything which carries this has been tested and assessed, and meets very stringent environmental criteria.

Just because a firm does not (yet) have an Eco-label for its products does not mean that they are not environmentally friendly. There are some well-established companies with a long track record and a lot of satisfied customers. Here are some key ones to look out for:

* **Ecover** are one of the oldest and largest of the green cleaning businesses.
* **Simple Green** have been supplying eco-friendly cleaning products for 30 years. Based in the US, they are now selling in the UK through their website at www.simplegreen.co.uk.
* **Cleen Green** are a small family firm based in the Midlands. They claim to be more driven by ethical and environmental consideration than by the desire to make money, and their prices reflect this.

Worth doing

Instead of buying commercial products, try using these natural substances for cleaning. They are non-toxic, bio-degradable, cheap, and effective!

* **Vinegar** – (preferably distilled, white vinegar). It is a mild acid, but strong enough to cut through grease, limescale and other types of dirt and stains. Vinegar can be used in a whole range of cleaning applications. Download *Great Uses of Vinegar* from TipKing at www.vinegarbook.net.

* **Lemon juice** – This is a stronger acid than vinegar, and can be used to tackle more stubborn stains, in place of bleach. The one big reservation about the use of lemons is that they all have to be imported, while vinegar can be produced from home-grown barley.
* **Baking soda** – (also known as bicarbonate of soda). Another highly adaptable cleaner, with many uses. It is a mild abrasive, and can be mixed to a thick paste with water for scrubbing heavily stained surfaces. It also has the useful property of absorbing smells. Check out TipKing's *Baking Soda Book* at www.bakingsodabook.co.uk.
* **Elbow grease** – A much under-rated resource. Sometimes all that's needed is water, a suitable brush and a bit of effort.

Ecoballs® are an alternative to soaps or detergents for washing clothes. They contain mineral salts which ionize the water, lowering surface tension so that it can penetrate deeper into fabrics. The balls are around £30 for a set of three, but will remain active for several hundred washes until the salt pellets finally dissolve completely – and they can then be refilled. Because there is no detergent present, less rinsing is needed, so a shorter wash cycle can be used. You won't need fabric conditioners either. All in all, they offer significant energy and environmental advantages. The only catch is that they don't cope with stains very well, so you will need to pre-treat stained clothes (with vinegar; see related text above).

Cleaning materials

There's a disposable culture in cleaning materials and it needs to change. Paper towels, even those made of recycled paper, represent a waste of resources and energy. And paper towels are not the only disposable cleaners. There are disposable dusters, toilet brushes, mops and cloths, sold on the promise that you can do it with one wipe. They are convenient, and – you don't have to deal with a filthy mop/brush/cloth/bucketful of water when you are done.

Worth doing

* Microfibre cloths are a long-life, reusable, machine-washable alternative. Used dry, or wet – and without any additional cleaning products – they can pick up both loose dust and dried-on dirt from surfaces. The trick, apparently, is in the microscopic size of the fibres which enables them to lift and retain dirt particles more effectively than cloths made with normal fibres.
* Natural sponges are a greener alternative to artificial sponges, and work just as well. When they reach the end of their life, they can be composted.

Household waste

Household waste has been a growing problem for a long time, but with growing awareness of the environmental and energy costs of waste and the rising cost of landfill, there is pressure on to reduce the amount we put into our bins. Local councils, have tackled the problem from the disposal end – setting up systems to encourage recycling. Most councils now supply householders with one or more additional bins for recyclable material, and we should make full use of these.

The following materials are all readily recyclable. If, for any reason, your council does not collect any of them, bag them up and drop them in at your nearest recycling centre when you are passing:

* glass
* paper and cardboard
* plastic bottles
* food/drink cans and aluminium trays
* textiles.

In theory all types of plastic are recyclable, but there are many different types and they must be separated before processing. At the moment, collection and separation costs outweigh the material value apart from plastic bottles.

Paints and varnishes

All standard paints and varnishes, even water-based ones, release volatile organic compounds (VOCs) – mostly during the initial drying phases, but continuing at a lower level for some long while after that. The levels vary immensely, and can be worryingly high. Fortunately, it is usually possibly to tell what the level will be, and to avoid the worst. Most paints and varnishes now carry a VOC label. There is no fixed standard for these, but they tend to follow the design shown here.

If 'High' on the label isn't enough for you, then read the safety warnings that you'll find elsewhere on the tin. High VOC paints and varnishes contain some quite noxious substances.

No-brainer

Avoid high and medium VOC finishes if at all possible – there are suitable low or medium VOC, water-based alternatives for most applications.

Disposing of paints and solvents

Oil and solvent-based paints, and white spirit, all count as hazardous substances and must be disposed of carefully. You shouldn't pour any of this stuff down the drain! Small quantities can be put into the domestic waste (sealed in plastic containers). Larger recycling centres often have paint collection points, or your council may collect it on request. Contact your council to find your local arrangements.

No-brainer

Reduce your disposal problems by only buying what you need. One litre of good quality emulsion paint will cover 6 square metres of wall with two coats – or 4 square metres if you need an extra coat to cope with bare plaster or a major colour change.

A litre of gloss paint will cover slightly less (around 5 square metres), but varnishes go further (up to 8 square metres).

Natural alternatives

* Clay paints are 100 per cent environmentally friendly – water-based, solvent-free, and containing only natural materials. Clay paint can be used in place of emulsion for walls and ceilings in living rooms and bedrooms. The range from Terrafino, one of the leaders in this market, consists of white, ochre, orange, red, brown and grey, but with each colour you can have anything from off-white to full strength. Have a look for yourself at www.tierrafino.com.
* Natural emulsions, such as those in the Aquamarijn range, use linseed and other vegetable oils as binding agents, and minerals as the pigments and fillers. The resulting finish is as washable as any ordinary emulsion. For more about these and other eco-friendly paints, visit Construction Resources at www.constructionresources.com.
* Gloss paints and varnishes can be made with plant oils – they all used to be until the last century! Thinners, for diluting paint or for cleaning brushes, can also be made from natural products such as citrus oil.

Furniture

There was a time when furniture was built to last, and was handed down from generation to generation. In this last half-century or so, we have become a throwaway society – we buy cheap then throw things away when they break or become tatty. This is not an ethical, environmentally friendly, resource-conscious way to do things. With furniture, as with so many things, the three Rs apply – we must learn to reduce, reuse and recycle.

Must-do

As far as possible, buy furniture and fittings made from recyclable or renewable materials.

You should only buy **wooden** furniture if it is made from reclaimed timber – which can be of better quality, texture and colour than new timber – or if it is grown in properly managed forests. Timber from certified sustainable sources carries a label. There are several of these, from different certification schemes, including those for new and recycled timber from the Forest Stewardship Council (FSC).

There can be ethical problems with **leather**. Clearly most vegans and vegetarians won't be buying leather furniture, but there are reasons why we should all think twice. Tanning can be highly polluting. The most widely used method is based on the use of chrome, but also uses sulphides and formaldehyde, among other toxic chemicals, and consumes over 10,000 gallons of water for every tonne of leather. In the developed world, tough environmental controls are in place to combat this pollution, but elsewhere tanning can be a major environmental and health problem.

Stainless steel is one thing that you can be fairly relaxed about. It is 100 per cent recyclable – and in fact, most of the stainless steel on the market today consists of 50 per cent recycled material. It is also extremely long-lasting, durable and very low maintenance – you will not need to use solvent cleaners or apply high VOC paint or varnish to it to keep it looking good.

Worth doing

Next time you need furniture, consider buying second-hand. It will extend the life of the item, and reduce the need for new ones to be made. Older, horse-hair stuffed chairs and sofas can be a real find, and well worth the cost of having them reupholstered.

And, of course, rather than junk your old furniture when you do need to get rid of it, put it up for sale, or donate it to one of the charity shops that handles furniture. Or freecycle it! (find out more at www.freecycle.org).

Floors and floor coverings

What are the greenest options for floor coverings? The answer to that depends upon what the floors are made of:

* Where there are **wooden floorboards**, the greenest covering is no covering. Sand the boards to remove old paint and varnish, if necessary, then seal with natural oils or varnish.
* Where a floor covering is needed, there's a good range of natural materials. For carpeting, apart from wool, there are also coir, seagrass, sisal and jute (add rugs where softness is needed). If you want wood flooring, choose solid timber or bamboo in preference to laminates. It is more expensive, but more durable.
* In kitchens and bathrooms, or wherever smooth, washable surfaces are needed, consider natural rubber or linoleum (real lino is made from linseed oil, resins, limestone, wood and jute – all natural and either renewable or very plentiful).

Possible suppliers:

* The Alternative Flooring Company at www.alternative-flooring.co.uk
* Construction Resources at www.constructionresources.com
* Dalsouple Rubber Flooring at www.dalsouple.com
* Upofloor parquet flooring at www.upofloor.com.

4

food and drink

In the UK, as in the rest of the developed world, we live in a time when food is cheap and plentiful, and when just about any type of foodstuff can be bought in the shops at more or less any time of the year. We eat better than kings did 50 years ago! But our eating and drinking habits are not sustainable and not ethical. There are three main issues:

* We are using far too much energy in the production and distribution of food and drink.
* Too many of the people who grow, pick, pack and sell our foods do not get a fair return for their labours.
* We are polluting the environment and ourselves with the chemicals used in growing and processing foods, and with discarded packaging and waste food.

Energy and food production

Mechanized farming and the liberal use of artificial fertilizers transformed food production in the twentieth century. A hundred years ago, one farmer could produce enough to feed three other people; now one farmer can feed over 100. But this is only achieved through massive inputs of energy, mainly from oil and gas. In peasant farming the ratio of input energy to output energy was over 1:40, but in modern, mechanized agriculture that drops to 1:1.3.

When you focus on protein production, the energy ratios go into the negatives – dramatically so with animal proteins. It takes a little over three units of fossil fuel energy to produce one unit of grain protein, and four units of energy for one of chicken protein, but for beef or lamb protein the ratio shoots up to 50:1.

Food miles

Fossil fuel input, of course, only *starts* at the farm. It then continues right down the supply chain, in its processing, packaging, storage and transportation. The distance food travels between the producer and your table is a crucial element in the total energy costs. This is sometimes expressed in 'food miles'. It's a crude measure – distance alone is not the only factor – but it does help to focus on energy costs, and to get people thinking more about local production and consumption.

Air miles

Air miles are the most marked aspect of this – 95 per cent of the fruit and 50 per cent of the vegetables in UK stores are imported. Much of this travels by sea or overland, and only 1 per cent by air – but that 1 per cent is responsible for over 10 per cent of the total food transport CO_2 emissions.

Some of this air-imported food is exotic, but much of it is unseasonal. We fly in French beans from Kenya, tomatoes from

Saudi Arabia, apples from South Africa, mushrooms from Zambia, baby sweetcorn from Thailand, asparagus from Peru – even Brussels sprouts from Australia. These can all be grown here in the UK, or close by in Europe, but only for part of the year.

Road miles

Our food travels a long way nowadays, on its route from the field to the plate. Fifty years ago, most vegetables and much meat would have gone from farmer to the local wholesale market then on to the local shops, perhaps travelling no more than 20 or 30 miles in total. Today, all but a tiny percentage of our food is sold through supermarkets, and that has had a major impact on road miles.

In 2005, the UK government commissioned a report into the *Validity of Food Miles as an Indicator of Sustainable Development*. It found that in 2002, transporting the UK's food took up a quarter of all HGV mileage within the UK and produced 10 million tonnes of CO_2. (It was also responsible for 19 million tonnes of CO_2 emissions in overseas road transport and air freight.) The report found that food transport was also responsible, each year, for over £9 billion of social and environmental costs, including congestion, accidents and infrastructure damage.

The report made a number of recommendations for how the government and the food industry could start to reduce the costs and impacts of road food transport, but the question for us is – What can we do as consumers? Can we reduce food miles?

The answer of course, is 'yes'. And we can have an impact at two levels.

1. Directly, we can reduce the food miles in our own groceries by changing our buying habits.
2. Indirectly, we can add to the pressure on the government and food industry to change their policies and practices – and we can do this through the shopping basket as well as in more active ways.

How can I reduce my food miles?

No-brainer

Use your small high street shops

Use your local greengrocers or butchers if you are lucky enough to have them. Small shops will normally get their supplies from the local wholesale market, which is where local growers sell their produce. And you won't just lower your food miles doing this, you will also:

* reduce packaging waste, as greengrocers tend to sell more loose and less pre-packed products
* help to keep your high street and its community alive.

Buy local-grown food

Whether you are shopping in the supermarket or the greengrocers, check the labels, or ask the shop staff, to find out where the produce was grown, and buy as local as you can. But 'local' has an elastic definition here. Strawberries grown in the same county are to be preferred over those from elsewhere in the UK, which are better than those from mainland Europe, which are better than those from further afield. Some fruits and vegetables have to come from a distance, but sea transport is very energy efficient – it uses less fuel to ship in a box of bananas from the Caribbean than to fly in a box of figs from Greece. Avoid buying anything brought in by air – do you really need Kenyan green beans and Thai baby sweetcorn?

Must-do

Eat more seasonal food

This is about eating what's in season in your locality, and we'll be stricter about 'local' here and limit it to the UK, or even to your county.

Eating local seasonal food will obviously reduce your food miles, but it also has other benefits. You will enjoy fruit and vegetables at their best, and at their freshest. It will help to tune you into the natural rhythms of the year. Salads and soft fruits make lighter meals for the warmth of summer days, while root vegetables and more solid greens give a solid heart to winter food.

You have to think more about your shopping and your diet if you decide that you are going to eat only seasonal foods, and it can be hard to persuade children – or adults – to change their eating habits overnight. If you have a family, work towards seasonal eating.

Seasonal food, month-by-month

One of the best websites for learning more about seasonal food is Eat the Seasons at www.eattheseasons.co.uk. They have a monthly guide to what's in season, with matching recipes, as well as articles on food and links to local and/or organic food producers, retailers and online suppliers.

Worth doing

Farm shops and farmers' markets

There are farmers' markets now throughout the UK, some open every week, others appearing monthly. It's a well-organized and supervised system. On a proper market – one approved by FARMA – the produce offered for sale must have been 'grown, reared, caught, brewed, pickled, baked, smoked or processed' by the stallholder, who lives and works in the local area. Prices tend to be a little higher than in the high street shops, but it's hard to find fresher fruit and vegetables, and the quality of the meat and other food products is normally very high.

There are currently over 1,000 FARMA certified farm shops in the UK, selling food grown or reared on the farm. Some of these are pick-your-own farms. Prices tend to be lower here, and of course you can know – to the minute – just how fresh your produce is!

Find out where and when the markets are in your area, and locate your local farm shops find them at www.farmersmarket.net.

Fresh to your door

If it is not convenient or practical for you to visit the local growers, they can come to you. Join a box scheme and have a box of fruit and vegetables delivered to your door each week. These are largely seasonal and mainly locally grown, and some schemes are only organic. The amount of control you have over the content will vary, according to the supplier, but it is going to be largely governed by the seasons, and you may have to adjust your eating habits to get the best out of your box. Treat the box as a challenge and an opportunity – what has nature's bounty delivered this week?

The people running these box schemes are mainly small farmers, many of whom already run farm shops or market stalls, and they will only deliver within a few miles of their base – the emphasis is on local sales of local produce. That should not present you with a problem. Box schemes have really taken off in the last few years, so that there are now very few places in the UK that are not within range of one or other deliverer. You can find the schemes running in your area at the Veg Box Schemes website (www.vegboxschemes.co.uk).

> If you would like to get involved in promoting the use of local foods, visit Sustain, the alliance for better food and farming, at www.sustainweb.org.

Grow your own

There is nothing quite like the taste of young carrots pulled, washed, cooked and eaten within half an hour, or cherry tomatoes eaten straight off the plant. It doesn't require great effort to enjoy your own produce – and to reduce your food miles. You can grow:

* herbs on a sunny windowsill
* herbs, tomatoes, peppers, chillies, strawberries, runner beans, salad greens and more in pots on a patio or balcony
* beans, peas, purple sprouting broccoli, and other vegetables with attractive foliage or flowers in the flower beds of a small garden
* a rich variety of vegetables, in short rows in a small plot – if stored carefully, seeds will remain good for several years.

Fish and meat

'Grow your own' is not a possibility for most of us when it comes to fish and meat. So what should we be looking for?

With fish, the key issue is sustainability. Over-fishing is threatening the existence of many species – scientists estimate that nearly 80 per cent of the world's fish stocks are in danger. In enclosed seas and inland waters, there is a realistic hope of controlling the level of fishing, but with deep-sea fishing, there is far less hope of the sort of international co-operation that would be needed to protect stocks.

Fish farming can be the answer, but it depends upon what sort of fish is being farmed and how. To rear salmon, for example, you need to feed them on a high-protein diet, and much of that currently comes from bottom-trawled fish, i.e. fish caught in nets that are dragged along the seabed, a very destructive type of trawling. So, salmon farming tends to increase over-fishing. Tilapia, on the other hand, is a herbivore and can be fed on plant-based foods and farmed sustainably.

If you really want to do this properly, you also need to take seasons into account, and the times of year when different sorts of fish are in season. The Marine Conservation Society runs the very helpful FishOnLine website at www.fishonline.org. They have handy lists of what fish you can eat, and what you should avoid.

With meat, the key issue is probably animal welfare. It's only fair, if you are going to eat an animal, that it should have had a decent quality of life up until the point of slaughter. Having respect for other creatures should be one of the things that make a decent human being, and at a lower level, free-range animals that have moved freely and used their muscles taste better.

No-brainer

Buy only free-range chickens (and eggs) and farm-reared, field-raised pork.

Worth doing

Join the campaign against factory farming. Visit www.factoryfarming.org.uk.

Organic food

The way that we grow food raises some major environmental concerns, ranging from the destruction of the Amazon rainforest to clear space for soya bean cultivation, to nitrate run-off in the waterways, with top soil erosion, the loss of biodiversity and much else in between. As consumers, it is hard for us to have much impact on many of these issues – though we can do more as campaigners – but we can encourage more sustainable, less damaging farming by buying more organic food.

What is organic?

Organic food is grown as naturally as possible, using no artificial fertilizers, herbicides, pesticides or growth hormones. The farming techniques are designed to be sustainable, keeping the soil in good condition, and using the minimum of fossil fuel energy. Animals must be fed on organic foodstuffs, have good living conditions and be spared unnecessary distress in transport and slaughter.

There is no single, absolute definition of 'organic', but in the UK the Soil Association is generally recognized as the leading body, and their accreditation carries most weight.

If food carries the Soil Association's symbol, it means that it has been produced to strict animal welfare and environmental standards. There are a number of aspects to this, and each is carefully defined. For example, to maintain fertility and soil quality, organic farmers will use crop rotation and can apply composts and manure, and certain natural mineral fertilizers. They cannot use artificial fertilizers which lack the trace elements needed for truly healthy crops, and which can inhibit the growth of the microbes that are needed for healthy soil.

Sales of organic food in the UK have boomed over the last few years, alongside the growth of the 'good food' culture and the increased enthusiasm for fitness and personal well being. Though they still account for a relatively small percentage of the total food market, organic food sales rose by 30 per cent in 2006 and have become much more mainstream, with all the supermarket chains now having organic sections. In keeping with the low-impact spirit of organic farming, most supermarkets now source at least part of their organic produce from local growers.

Worth doing

Organic foods are normally more expensive than the conventional alternative, but are free from the herbicide and pesticide residues which may be damaging to us in the long term. Organic farming is, by definition, sustainable, in contrast to conventional agriculture that is dependent upon heavy inputs of energy – primarily from fossil fuels. For our own personal good, and to help ensure future food supplies for us all, we should buy more organic foods.

Do I have to go vegan to be ethical?

Well, if you want to be truly ethical, the answer is probably 'yes'. It certainly ticks all the boxes.

Currently a substantial amount of the world's crops go to animal feed to produce meat for the wealthier countries. If no one ate meat, the world would be able to produce more than enough food to keep everyone well fed.

We noted earlier how much more fossil fuel energy goes into producing meat compared with crops. A meatless diet would reduce fuel use and CO_2 emissions.

You don't have to be an animal rights activist to recognize that not all animals are reared, or transported or slaughtered in ideal conditions. If you are a vegan, no animal is suffering on your behalf.

Eating less meat has got to be better for the environment. Ensuring that the meat you do eat is ethically reared and slaughtered is essential. Organic is preferable.

Food waste

Recent research showed that in the UK, on average, we throw away one-third of the food we buy, and that half of this is still fit to eat. This represents not just a waste of money by individuals, but also a huge waste of resources for society as a whole. If we could eliminate most of that waste, we could cut our total CO_2 emissions by 5 per cent or more, take 1 in 10 HGVs off the roads, and save a lot of landfill.

Food waste should not go into landfill because it rots, producing methane, and leachate – toxic liquid. Local councils and the food industry are exploring more eco-friendly ways to deal with food waste. Composting is a good use for raw vegetable waste, meat and processed foods can be converted to bio-fuel and/or used for electricity generation. These initiatives are to be encouraged. Find out what your local council is doing, and if they aren't doing anything special with food wastes, ask why not. You might like to point them in the direction of Inetec, who develop large-scale waste management systems – visit them at www.inetec.co.uk to find out more.

The charity Fareshare runs a community food network that collects unwanted food – surplus, or near or past its 'best before' date – from shops and businesses. If you would like to get involved, contact them through the website at www.fareshare.org.uk.

Restaurants and food processors produce something like 100,000 tonnes of used cooking oil a year, but this is increasingly recognized as a resource rather than as a disposal problem. It can be purified, refined and converted into animal feed or bio-diesel, or used in the manufacture of soap and cosmetics. A few councils run cooking oil collection services for householders. If this is not available in your area, cooking oil can be added to the compost, but otherwise should go (in a bottle) into the bin.

Reducing your food waste

We can all reduce the amount of food that we throw away, and we can do so very easily. The following suggestions could all be listed as 'no-brainers' – in that there is no question that these are good things to do – but they do require a little thought!

Must-do

* Only buy what you need. Think ahead to the meals that you will be preparing between now and the next shopping trip.
* Eat before you shop. It's harder to resist impulse buying when you are hungry.
* Avoid value packs and '2 for 1' offers on fresh produce unless you can freeze what you don't need immediately.

* Store fresh food in the fridge, and check that its temperature is 5° or below.
* Keep an eye on the dates. Remember that 'best before' means precisely that. 'Use by' does mean use by the given date, so plan ahead and make sure that you do.
* Weigh and measure when you are cooking, and keep leftovers to a minimum.

Worth doing

Raw kitchen waste, including vegetable peelings, outer leaves, skins, tea bags and coffee grounds, and all manner of garden waste – weeds, prunings, grass cuttings and the like – can be turned into compost and used to enrich the soil. You don't even need a garden – there are small, closed systems that you can use indoors.

Traditional compost heaps

These do need a garden, because you need some space and you need exposed soil. There is a minimum size for effective composting. The heap needs to be half a metre or so in every dimension to generate enough heat in the middle for vegetable matter to break down fully. A simple heap on the ground will eventually turn into compost, but you get much better results, faster, if the waste matter is enclosed in something to keep the rain off and to retain heat, which encourages the essential bacterial action.

At the simplest, you can just chuck your kitchen and garden waste in the top, then start to shovel compost out of the bottom next year. You will get a better quality of compost, and in a shorter time, if you take a little more care over what goes in and how. You need a mixture of:

* wet, green material such as kitchen waste, plant prunings and grass cuttings, which provide nitrogen and rot quickly

and

* drier fibrous matter such as fallen leaves, paper or cardboard to improve the structure and let the heap breathe, but rot relatively slowly.

A layer of ordinary soil every now and then will also help to balance the mix.

Wormeries

Wormeries are closed containers that rely on the action of worms to turn kitchen waste into compost. Designs vary, but typically there are several layers of trays with mesh bottoms, above a collection tray with a tap.

If you want to know more about composting, and to find out about low-cost bins, visit the home composting page at recycle now (www.recyclenow.com/home_composting).

The process is much faster than traditional composting – you're talking six weeks from waste to compost, not six months – and you can get totally closed containers which are suitable for patios or even indoor use.

Food packaging

The basic problems with food packaging are the waste of resources it causes and its disposal – a third of household waste is food packaging, adding up to a total of over 6 million tonnes a year in the UK, and most of this goes to landfill where it will decay slowly over the next few hundred years.

Reducing your packaging waste

No-brainer

* Don't add to the packaging problem. Bunches of bananas, melons and pineapples do not need to go into plastic bags – they have their own natural wrappings. So for that matter do cabbages, cauliflowers and lettuces.
* Where there is a choice, buy the ones with least packaging or with recyclable packaging.
* Don't buy individually wrapped portions. A pack of six yogurts has a much lower content to plastic ratio than one large pot. Buy a big pot and transfer to a small glass jar or

reusable plastic pot if small portions are needed for lunch boxes.

Worth doing

* Use your local milkman. You will pay a little more per pint, but the glass bottles can be reused continuously, and having milk delivered to your door, normally in an electric vehicle, you may be able to reduce your trips (by car) to the shops, and therefore lower your food miles.
* Find out more about how you can help to reduce packaging by visiting the WRAP (Waste & Resources Action Programme) website at www.wrap.org.uk.

Fairtrade

By historic standards, food is very cheap in the UK. Falling prices have been partly the result of better productivity, economies of scale and a more efficient distribution system, but they have also dropped because supermarkets have used their huge buying power to drive down the prices they pay farmers. That is a problem for farmers and farm workers in this country, but even more so in developing countries. Too many small farmers and plantation workers growing bananas, pineapples, coffee, tea, sugar cane, avocados and other fruits and tropical products, are not getting a living wage from their work. Too many poor communities are becoming more impoverished as they labour to put cheap food on our supermarket shelves.

The Fairtrade movement was started to fight this injustice. It aims to ensure that the growers get a fair share of the profit from their produce, and that their communities begin to lift themselves out of poverty. Fairtrade products are not necessarily more expensive than unfairly traded ones – the difference is that more of the profits go to the growers, and less to the middlemen and retailers.

The Fairtrade Foundation is the main campaigning and certifying body for Fairtrade. Any produce which carries its symbol has to meet very clear standards. In a Fairtrade deal, farmers are guaranteed a price above the normal market price for their crop which is set for several years, so that they can plan for the long term. No matter how the world market price drops, the farmers will never be paid below the agreed minimum price, but if it rises, they will get a premium above the going rate. The buyer is also required to invest in the local community, helping to pay for schools or health care.

The banana rip-off

In 2007, *The Guardian* commissioned an analysis of the profits of the big fruit firms – Dole, Chiquita, Del Monte and Fyffes – who between them control over 75 per cent of the global market in bananas. This showed how little of the profit went to the grower. When you spend £1 on bananas in the supermarket, 40p goes to the store, 48p goes to the supplier and 12p is taken by the production costs, and of this labour costs form only 1.5p. But it's not just the workers on the plantations and in the packaging plants that are getting ripped off. The fruit firms all work through networks of companies, mainly based in tax havens, and they arrange their costs so that the profits are concentrated where the tax rates are lowest or non-existent. These firms typically pay little tax in the countries where the fruit is grown, little where it is sold, and little in their home country – in fact, they pay very little tax anywhere.

You do not have to contribute to their profits. Fairtrade bananas give a good price to the farm workers, and are shipped by more ethical businesses. Of the supermarkets, Sainsbury's and Waitrose sell only Fairtrade bananas, the Co-op has been selling Fairtrade bananas for some time, and more recently Tesco and Asda have come on board. Consumer choices and campaigning pressure are steadily winning this battle.

No-brainer

If there are equivalent Fairtrade and non-Fairtrade products on the shelf, buy Fairtrade.

Worth doing

* If your supermarket (or greengrocer) does not sell Fairtrade goods, ask why not – then go elsewhere to buy them.
* Find out more about the work of the Fairtrade Foundation. Visit them at www.fairtrade.org.uk.

Bottled water

Bottled water represents one of marketing's greatest triumphs over common sense. In the developed world, where most of it is drunk, tap water is better regulated, less likely to contain contaminants, and often tastes better than bottled water – if your tastebuds are sensitive enough to notice the difference. In the developing world, where public tap water may be of more varying quality and purity, the availability of bottled water (for those that can afford it) reduces the pressure on governments to make sure that a safe water supply is there for everyone.

Bottled water is bad for the environment. It is estimated that in manufacturing and transporting the plastic bottle, extracting and processing the water and transporting the filled bottle, around 1 litre of oil is used for every 4 litres of water. And 5 litres of water – 6 litres if it is imported – is used to manufacture and transport each litre of bottled water. Further to this, around 90 per cent of the empty bottles are thrown out with the general rubbish, to finish up in landfill.

Don't buy bottled water. If you need a bottle of water when you go out, fill your own bottle from your own tap. If you want cold bottled water when you are out, fill a bottle from the tap the day before and keep it in the fridge.

5

shopping and money matters

This is something of a catch-all chapter, to cover things which are not covered elsewhere, but there are common themes. The main one, of course, is that we need to follow the three Rs – reduce, reuse, recycle. If you don't really need it, don't buy it. If you do really need one, would second-hand do? And when you no longer need it, put it back into circulation for reuse, or make sure that its components get recycled. Energy use is another issue. The clothes, soft furnishings, toys, gadgets and similar small items in our shops all take energy to manufacture, and most are imported, racking up a lot of fuel miles – though mainly by sea, which is more carbon efficient than either land or air transport. Finally, there are the human costs. A high proportion of these goods are produced in poor working conditions with low rates of pay.

Buy less – or even, buy nothing

For years our basic problem has been that we have been buying too much – too many clothes, gadgets, toys, books (did you buy this copy, or – environmentally better – borrow it from a friend or the library?) and everything else. If we all bought less, it would reduce the strain on the environment and we might even be the happier for it. By late 2008, total credit card debt in the UK had risen to over £200 billion – and that did not include mortgages, which then totalled over £1.2 trillion. In the USA, total personal debt – again not counting mortgages – was close to $2 trillion. After the bank crashes and subsequent credit crunch, the levels of debt have been rising much more slowly, and may even be starting to fall. If we spent less and had less debt hanging over us, wouldn't we be happier?

Look out for this year's Buy Nothing Day – you can get details from the website at www.buynothingday.co.uk – and take the spirit of the movement to heart and try to restrict your purchases all year round. How many coats, pairs of shoes, jumpers do you really need? (I suspect that men will find these questions easier to answer than women.) Do you really need to replace your solar-powered mobile phone charger with a new one that's 10 per cent more efficient? (And women will find it easier to say 'No' to that.)

Clothes

There are two key questions we need to ask about clothes: How were they manufactured? What materials are they made from?

Fair wages

In the last two decades, the supermarket approach to retailing – pile them high and sell them cheap – has extended across into clothes. For the customer, this has meant much cheaper clothes; for the manufacturers it is a different story. In Sri Lanka, for example, prices paid to clothes factories have dropped 30 per cent in the last ten years, but those factories have faced a 20 per cent increase in costs for raw materials and energy. There are two ways in which manufacturers can produce more for less: improve the efficiency of the factory by installing new machines and/or adopting better work practices; make the workers do more, for less. The second approach is taken all too often, and we – the shoppers in the West – are part of this exploitation. If price is a major factor in where we buy clothes, retailers will compete to sell at lower prices, and they will get their price cuts by paying their suppliers less. The big chain stores and supermarkets buy in huge quantities, but only on limited contracts, and are willing and able to switch to alternative suppliers at the drop of a T-shirt.

Labour Behind the Label has been campaigning on behalf of garment workers for some years. Find out how you can help by visiting them at www.labourbehindthelabel.org.

Materials

The basic assumption that natural must be best isn't necessarily true. **Cotton** is a prime example. It is one of the most water-intensive and environmentally damaging products. Developing countries use around 300,000 tonnes of pesticides each year, and half of this goes on cotton alone – and that works out at half a cupful for every T-shirt! This is destroying eco-systems and killing people. (To find out more about this problem, visit PAN at www.pan-uk.org.)

Growing and processing both require huge quantities of water – in total about 1,000 litres per T-shirt. Competition for water is already a problem in many parts of Africa, the Middle East and Asia, and the scale and scope of the problem is increasing.

Organic cotton – is a big step forward, but not the end of the road. It really needs to be Fairtrade grown, unbleached and/or naturally dyed. The dyes are probably the biggest sticking point. Natural, vegetable dyes tend to have a limited colour range, but what's more of a problem is that the colorant is such a small part of the plant that you need to grow a lot to get a little dye, which makes it very expensive.

Hemp fibres are tough enough to be made into rope, but can be soft and fine enough to be made into lace; used by itself or combined with cotton, silk or other textiles, it can be spun into yarn for knitting or woven into fabrics. The plant's seeds are a good source of proteins and oils; the woody core can be used for paper-making; and anything left over can be burnt as biomass fuel or converted to bio-diesel or ethanol.

Bamboo is a textile that people are just beginning to appreciate. It has all the advantages of cotton, and more, and does not have cotton's environmental costs. Bamboo fibres are hollow and much thinner than cotton fibres, producing fabrics that are very soft, and breathable, wicking moisture away from the skin. They are also antibacterial, antifungal and offer a high level of UV protection.

Linen is the most ancient of all fabrics, going back at least 5,000 years. It is produced from flax, which grows faster than cotton and requires considerably less fertilizers or pesticides. The production process also requires fewer chemicals.

Unwanted clothing

Old clothes are a valuable resource. If there's life left in a garment, there's probably someone, somewhere, who would be happy to wear it. Clothes may become unwanted after very little wear – children grow out of things, and adults change shape (intentionally or otherwise); garments may be bought for specific occasions, and have no purpose afterwards. The charity shops do a sterling job of recycling clothing, with very little going to waste. Garments which are likely to sell in their shops go onto the rails; others, which are wearable but no longer sellable, are collected for shipment out to Third World countries. And those which are really beyond wear are sent on to reclamation companies who can find a use for most types of fabrics. Woollen garments can be reduced to fibres for reworking into new yarn; cotton and silk are made into wiping rags for industry, or used in paper-making; some are chopped to make felt for insulating and lining – there's very little wasted.

How can I dress greener?

No-brainer

* **Don't buy cheap clothes** made in Third World sweatshops. Visit Let's Clean Up Fashion (www.labourbehindthelabel.org)

before you start shopping, and support those stores that are trying hardest to ensure that their garments are produced ethically.

* **Don't throw away clothes** when they are no longer wanted. If they are wearable, donate them to a charity shop or swap or sell them through a clothes exchange. If they are really worn out, those made from absorbent fabrics can be cut up into rags and used in place of paper kitchen towels.

Worth doing

* **Buy organic** – It's the environmentally friendly thing to do. You can find a comprehensive list of retailers at About Organics (www.aboutorganics.co.uk) – look for the Organic Clothing link.
* **Buy second-hand** – You would be surprised at what turns up. And sales of clothing are an important source of income for many charities.
* **Buy to last** – Choose garments that will wear well, and that you will want to wear for a long time.
* **Buy recycled** – Or rather, buy clothes with some recycled content, if possible. At the moment there is no standard labelling system to indicate this, so you cannot always tell.

Gadgets

There are lots of gadgets on offer for the environmentally aware – solar-powered battery chargers, wind-up radios, water-powered batteries, smart sockets that turn themselves off when an appliance goes on standby, foot-powered electricity generators.

Must-do

Three questions to ask before buying any of these:

1 Will you actually use it? Because if an energy-saving device is not used, then the energy that went into its manufacture has been wasted.

2 Does it serve a useful purpose?
3 If you are buying gadgets as gifts, will the recipients use them, and are they likely to already have them?

The crucial point is that much of our current trouble stems from over-consumption. The way out has to be by buying less, not buying more – gadgets, in particular, should be looked at with a very critical eye.

Gifts

Being ethical does not have to mean being joyless. The art of giving is an important part of social bonding – and receiving gifts is a pleasure. Let's try and give ethically.

* **Buy Fairtrade.** Buying goods from Third World producers at fair prices helps them to build their future – and you get a quality product.
* **Give a donation.** Several charities run donations-as-gifts schemes, where you pay for a specific item, to be given in the recipient's name. You will then have a card to give to the other person telling them about the donation. What your recipient gets out of it is a nice warm feeling. Traidcraft (www.traidcraftshop.co.uk) offers a limited number of 'Gifts for life'; Oxfam (www.oxfam.org.uk) has a much wider range of donations in their 'Unwrapped' selection.
* **Give a loan.** This is similar to giving a donation, except that here you can make an interest-free loan to a specific person in a developing country, to help them to expand or to get a business off the ground. As the loans are almost always repaid in full and on time, all that you lose is the interest. Find out more at www.kiva.org.

Plastic shopping bags

We get through a staggering number of plastic shopping bags every year – estimates range from 12 to 18 billion plastic bags just from the supermarkets. That's upwards of 200 bags per person per year! Why do we use so many? And where do they all go?

We use them because they are there and we are too lazy to think ahead and take bags with us when we go shopping.

Most plastic bags currently finish up in landfill – though some blow around the streets and countryside, or clog the rivers and seas. Less than 1 per cent of plastic bags are currently recycled. They all could be.

We don't actually need disposable plastic shopping bags. In fact, there are whole countries that are managing without them.

The question is, what to use in place of thin, single-use plastic bags? One solution is thick, reusable plastic bags. They have been in use in the UK for some years now, but only carry a small percentage of the shopping home. Why? Because the supermarkets are still giving away thin ones. If there are no free bags, and the choice is between buying new 'bags for life' or remembering to bring your old ones with you – as happens in French supermarkets – people bring bags.

No-brainer

Buy yourself enough shopping bags – preferably made from natural materials such as cotton or jute, but otherwise long-lasting plastic 'bags for life' – to cope with your shopping habits and remember to take them with you (that's the tricky bit until it becomes ingrained).

Worth doing

Start a campaign to turn your town or local high street into a plastic-bag-free zone. You can find out how Modbury did it at their website www.modbury.net.

Ethical shopping guides

Ethical Company Organisation – www.ethical-company-organisation.org

This looks at the companies, not just the goods, matching them to ethical and environmental criteria, and giving comparative information on literally thousands of companies and brands. It publishes the *Good Shopping Guide*, a valuable reference book if you are serious about who you shop and do business with, and also runs the gooshing site:

gooshing – www.gooshing.co.uk

This is a shopping guide, ranking goods mainly on ethical rating of the companies that produce them.

The Green Providers Directory – www.search-for-me.co.uk

A comprehensive directory of firms offering green, organic and Fairtrade products and services.

Guide me green – www.guidemegreen.com

A UK-based directory of green companies, covering accommodation, food, travel, magazines and charities as well as retailers.

A lot of organics – www.alotoforganics.co.uk

UK organic directory and search engine, covering a full spectrum of organic producers, retailers and other organizations.

Money

Money may or may not be the root of all evil, but it can certainly be put to evil purposes. Our concern should be to ensure that our money is used to support only environmentally friendly, people-friendly, peaceful, fair purposes. Because our money is actively used, whether we are aware of it or not. The money held in our accounts – current or savings – and the money we pay into our private/company pension fund is being loaned or invested by the banks and pension funds in all manner of ways. We can take control of this, and make sure that our money is only used for ethical purposes.

Banking

This is an area where the choice is very, very simple. There is only one UK bank that operates and invests according to strict ethical conditions, and offers the full range of banking services to personal customers. That bank is the Co-operative. This is part of the wider Co-operative Wholesale Society, and its members have always been strong on issues of peace, justice and fair dealing. In 1991 the bank found that the majority of its customers would welcome a clear ethical policy on investments. One was introduced, initially banning loans to any companies involved in the arms trade or human rights violations in any form, and supporting organizations with socially useful purposes. It has continued to consult its customers regularly, to ensure that its ethical policy reflects their concerns.

The Bank is also working hard to reduce its own environmental impact, and publishes an annual Sustainability Report setting out its economic, social and ecological targets, and how much progress it has made over the year.

If you want a current account with a truly ethical bank, the choice is then very simple: do you choose a branch-based account with the Co-operative Bank, or an online account with Smile, the Co-operative Movement's internet bank? Internet banking is not convenient if you need to pay in cheques or cash regularly, but it does offer better interest rates on its savings and current account.

The other ethical banks

There are two other ethical banks operating in the UK, but neither provides the full banking service to personal customers.

Triodos, a Netherlands-based company, offers only savings accounts to individuals, as its focus is ethical businesses. For these it provides the full range of current accounts, savings and loans (Triodos is Cafédirect's banker, and rightly proud of it). It also has a venture capital arm that specializes in finance for solar and wind energy projects, organic farming and similar developments. Find out more about Triodos on the web at www.triodos.co.uk.

The Charity Bank is a registered charity which is also a bank. Its purpose is to provide low-interest loans for charitable activities, and it takes deposits from people who are happy to know that their money is doing good, even though it may be earning less interest than it could have earned elsewhere. The bank normally pays up to 2 per cent interest, though it did initially take deposits into its CITRA (Community Investment Tax Relief) fund which, with tax relief actually worth 7 per cent a year, was better than ordinary bank accounts.

Find out more about their work and how you can put your money to work ethically, at www.charitybank.org.

In the USA, Wainwright Bank & Trust Company works to very similar ethical principles, as does Grupo Financiero FINSOL in Mexico, GLS bank in Germany and Banca Popolare Etica, in Italy and Spain.

Islamic banking

Islamic banking is based on the values behind Shariah law, which aims to protect the five 'pillars' of an Islamic society – faith, life, wealth, intellect and posterity. Shariah law bans paying or receiving interest, but permits the payment of dividends on shares. An Islamic bank will not invest in any company which is involved in alcohol, tobacco, gambling, armaments, pornography, pork or finance (which could be charging interest or investing in unacceptable activities).

You do not have to be a Muslim to use an Islamic bank. For more information contact the Institute of Islamic Banking and Insurance at www.islamic-banking.com.

Mortgages

Apart from the Co-operative Bank, the most ethical source of mortgages at present must be the **Ecology Building Society**. This was set up just over 25 years ago to promote sustainable housing and provides mortgages only for ecologically beneficial, energy-efficient housing or renovation projects. They carry their commitment to sustainability through into their own offices and practices, and their care for people is shown in their attitude to borrowers. They will not lend more than three times earnings, because they do not want people to be over-stretched.

If you are looking for a mortgage for a new build, a conversion or for buying woodlands or even a houseboat mooring, then find out more about them at www.ecology.co.uk.

Ethical investment

At the time of writing, the stock market is still reeling from the bank failures of 2008, giving investors a sharp reminder that shares can go down as well as up, but ethical investments have generally fared better than the rest of the market. On average, shares in UK companies are down nearly 40 per cent from the market's peak in mid-2007, but those in ethical funds have tended to lose less value.

One of the key organizations in the ethical investment field is EIRIS, Ethical Investment Research Services, which was set up in 1983 by a group of charities and churches who wanted to ensure that their own investments met ethical criteria. You can find out more about their work and get general advice on ethical investment at their website, www.eiris.org.

Ethical Investors Group is ethical in more than just name – these people are top of the *Guardian*'s Giving List, donating 50 per cent of their pre-tax profits to charities (compared with the 1–2 per cent that most companies manage). They give advice on pensions, mortgages, ISAs and insurance.

To read more, go to the Ethical Investors Group at www.ethicalinvestors.co.uk and follow the link to the Ethical Fund Directory.

There are many other financial advisers who are willing to give advice on ethical investment. You will find a directory of them at the Ethical Investment Association www.ethicalinvestment.org.uk.

6

travel and transport

We have become a mobile society. Millions of us commute to work or drive our children to school every day; we routinely travel – sometimes long distances – to see our scattered families; we expect to take overseas holidays, perhaps several times a year. The greater part of this travel is by car, and almost all transport is powered by oil. Travel and transport is hugely polluting and one of the main factors behind global warming. We cannot continue to live this way – if we do, oil will become too expensive to burn within the next generation. We need to drive a lot less, and to be far more efficient when we do drive; we need to fly a lot less, and to import a lot less by air. We need to be far more aware of our impact on the planet when choosing our holidays.

Motoring

Cars are a blessing and a curse. They have given us the freedom to travel where we will, but at huge environmental costs – global warming, air pollution, noise nuisance, and the destruction of the landscape with ribbons of tarmac are just the worst of these costs.

CO_2 emissions are probably the single most urgent of these problems. Road transport is currently responsible for almost a quarter of the total CO_2 emissions in the UK, and around 15 per cent of the total worldwide. These figures have increased dramatically in the last 25 years, and are expected to continue to increase for some time. In 1980, the 12 million or so cars and taxis on Britain's roads travelled 140 billion miles a year; in 2010 nearly 35 million cars and taxis in the UK, clock over 300 billion miles between them. That's just in the UK, and it doesn't include trucks and lorries. Globally, the total number of motor vehicles is expected to top 1 billion by 2025, and they will be discharging nearly 2,000 million tonnes of CO_2 into the atmosphere.

Air pollution is the second most pressing problem. Vehicles are responsible for a very large part of most pollutant emissions, especially in cities. In London, 99 per cent of carbon monoxide, 90 per cent of hydrocarbons and 76 per cent of nitrogen oxides are produced by traffic. Where levels of particulates (fine dust and soot) are high, road traffic is typically responsible for 75–85 per cent of this.

According to the Department of Health, the deaths of between 12,000 and 24,000 people a year are accelerated by air pollution.

Do you really need your car?

The first and most essential question you need to ask yourself is: 'Do I really need a car?' Will public transport, walking, cycling, perhaps with the occasional taxi and car hire, do the job? In the UK, the reality of public transport is that you are probably only going to be able to answer 'yes' to this second question if you live in London or another big city. The further you get into the countryside, the more difficult life becomes without a car. But do think about it – and do the sums. If you do not use your car much, the ongoing costs of maintenance, tax, insurance and depreciation add significantly to the average cost per mile. It can get to a point where it is cheaper to dispose of the car and hire a taxi for those journeys where public transport and muscle power won't do.

Two figures to bear in mind when looking at your mileage costs and annual costs:

* taxis currently cost about £2.40 a mile
* you can hire a car from £20 a day.

Fuel consumption and pollution are not the only issues. As well as having to be refuelled constantly, a car must first be manufactured, from raw and processed materials, then transported to its point of sale, repaired and maintained throughout its life, and disposed of at the end. You need to look at use of resources and energy over the whole of its lifespan and the environmental impact of disposal.

In practice, ethics are rarely the only consideration in how we choose and use a car. We all have to travel to a greater or lesser extent. What varies are the distance, the number of people that are travelling together, the quantity of equipment to be carried with the people, the feasibility of public transport, and other factors. These determine whether or not a car must be used, and what size and type of car.

Working with what you've got

If you have to have a car, the least you can do is to try to maximize your miles per gallon (mpg) and minimize your CO_2 and noxious emissions – fuel-efficient driving is the 'no-brainer' and the 'must-do' here.

Before you start

Travel light

Don't carry anything that you don't need on that journey.

Rack off

Roof racks and boxes create turbulence over the car, increasing drag and wind resistance. Even an unloaded rack will increase fuel consumption by 2 to 3 per cent.

Pump up

Under-inflated tyres increase fuel consumption – 1 per cent extra for every 6 psi under the proper pressure – and they wear out faster, so that's a double cost to you and the environment.

Keep it in good condition

Regular maintenance and servicing is crucial for best efficiency.

Plan the trip

Decide if it is really necessary. Do you have to pop down to the shops/library/post office/Aunty Edna's today? Do you need to see that client/supplier/consultant face-to-face, or could it be done over the phone or internet?

Is the car the best way to get there? How long will it take compared with public transport? And how does the cost of petrol and parking compare with the fare?

If you must go, pick your time and your route to get the smoothest run. A steady 60 or 65 mph on a good road or motorway gives you better mpg than accelerating and braking on country roads or struggling through congestion in towns.

Can you share the journey with anyone else?

On the road

Go with the flow

Relax, don't get stressed, enjoy the ride, and take your time. Just about all of the techniques for good, safe, fuel-efficient driving flow from this. Aggressive driving uses more fuel and puts more wear on the tyres, brakes, suspension and engine.

Drive with a light foot

Accelerating and braking gently reduces wear on the brakes and engine, and can improve fuel efficiency by up to 30 per cent.

Use your gears properly

Engines normally deliver their most fuel-efficient performance when turning over at between 2,000 and 3,000 rpm. Above – and below – this, you are using more fuel per mile.

Turn off when stationary

If you are likely to be stationary for more than a minute or so, turn off the engine.

Don't hang about

Once you've started the engine, go. You don't need to wait for it to warm up, but do drive gently at first until the engine has reached its normal running temperature.

But take your time

The optimum speed for fuel use varies with vehicles and driving conditions but is in the range 50–60 mph.

But slower isn't necessarily more economical – 45 mph in fifth gear gives better mpg than 40 mph in fourth. Ticking over in top is the ideal speed.

Use the ventilation system

Air conditioning, increases fuel consumption, and this is worse at slower speeds – it can add up to 11 per cent to fuel use. Open windows increase drag – and hence fuel use. The impact can be as much as 6 per cent. Try to use the ventilation system alone for cooling your car.

Total energy costs

A car-less life may be the ethical ideal, but for most of us a car is a necessity, given our lifestyles. (And changing our lifestyles is something that we should always be willing to consider.) What car should you buy? The answer has to be the most fuel-efficient one that will meet your requirements, and this will generally be the smallest one that will do the job, and the one that offers the best mpg in its class. But this is not always the case.

Dust to dust

In 2004 and 2005, CNW Marketing Research Inc undertook a major study to try to assess the total lifetime 'dust to dust' cost of vehicles in terms of energy usage – and they really did mean 'total'. The energy costs included not only that used in the plant to manufacture the vehicle, but also the energy costs of extracting and processing the raw materials, of employees getting to work, of shipping vehicles to the dealers, of making and fitting spare parts, right through to the costs of disposal and scrapping. The costs were then worked to produce an energy cost per mile, expressed in dollars based on 2005 oil prices. There were, of course, all sorts of assumptions in calculating these figures, but the same methodology was applied throughout and this was an independent study (it was not sponsored by any sector of the automotive industry, and indeed the researchers went to some pains to ensure that the manufacturers did not realize that the study was in progress).

Some of the results were much as you might expect. The most energy-expensive vehicle was the Mercedes Maybach (a 6-litre, 6-metre-long, 12-mpg limo) at $11.58 per mile; the least expensive was the Scion xB (a small Toyota, built purely for the US market) at $0.48 cents. What was more surprising at first sight was that the hybrids did not come out that well, in terms of overall energy consumption. For example, the conventional Honda Accord was assessed at $2.18 energy per mile, but the Hybrid version came out at $3.30 – nearly 50 per cent higher. This was due to higher manufacturing and research and development energy costs, and an expected relatively short working life.

The other real surprise was that while SUV (sports utility vehicles, which we call 4 × 4s) may have poor fuel economy, their overall costs are not that high. For example, the Hummer H3 (a big one!) was assessed at only $1.95 per mile. Why? For the same reason as the poor score of the hybrids, but at the other ends of the scales:

* Simplicity of manufacture and of repair.
* They clock-up high mileages – an average of 270,000.
* They last for years.
* SUVs use well-established technology, so R&D costs are tiny.

Alternative fuels

The ideal fuels are electricity or hydrogen, as long as both are derived using renewable technology. But neither of these – as yet – is suitable for mass-market, main-use cars. We'll come back to both of them later, after we have looked at petrol, diesel and their possible alternatives.

Petrol and diesel

The combustion of petrol and diesel is a major contributor to global warming, and we should reduce our use on those grounds alone; but there is another and more commanding reason to cut down. Both are derived from crude oil, and there's a finite supply of that. Globally, oil production has probably peaked – from here on out, it's going to get scarcer and more expensive.

Liquefied Petroleum Gas (LPG)

LPG is a mixture of propane and butane and burns cleaner than petrol or diesel. A petrol engine can be modified to run on LPG, and though this will cost something over £1,500, LPG is about half the price of petrol, so that running costs are dramatically lower.

You can find out more about the practicalities of switching to LPG at www.autogas.ltd.uk, the website of AutoGas, the UK's leader in this market.

Ethanol and flexi-fuel

Ethanol is a form of alcohol produced by fermenting vegetable matter. In Brazil, the world's largest producer of ethanol, they use sugar cane as the feedstock, but any plant material – including domestic vegetable waste – can be used. It is a clear burning fuel, with a high octane rating, which delivers good efficiency. You can run cars on pure ethanol, but in Europe it is usually blended with petrol for use in 'flexi-fuel vehicles' (FFVs) which can also run on pure petrol if they can't find an ethanol filling station.

Bio-diesel

Bio-diesel is a substitute for diesel produced from plant sources, such as palm oil, rape seed, and sunflowers. Like ethanol it is, in theory, carbon neutral and renewable, and cars running on it produce fewer toxic emissions – no sulphur dioxide, half as much soot and particulates, up to 50 per cent less carbon monoxide, and anything up to 95 per cent less hydrocarbons.

Governments have leapt on bio-diesel as a voter-friendly way to 'fight climate change', and are promoting it with a variety of tax incentives. In the UK, bio-diesel currently costs about half as much as standard diesel, and is effectively free of tax for private motorists. But there is a real question as to how far bio-diesel really is environmentally friendly, and whether it is actually carbon neutral.

The costs of bio-diesel

You need very large areas of land to grow sufficient crops to meet the oil needs of modern economies, and the problem lies in what is being displaced from that land. If crops are grown for fuel, rather than consumption, it can increase food costs.

In Europe, currently less than 1.5 per cent of fuels are bio-fuels. In 2006, an EU directive was agreed that would have required this to rise to 5.75 per cent by 2012, and 10 per cent by 2020, but by 2008 doubts about the environmental costs of bio-fuels have lead to a rethink of the policy. These targets could not be met with locally produced bio-fuels – you would have to turn over a quarter of Europe's arable land to fuel crops to do that – they need imported fuels.

We are exporting our problems with bio-fuels as we are with so many of our environmental problems. In Indonesia and the Philippines, large swathes of forest are being cleared for palm oil plantations, for bio-diesel production. The destruction of habitats is endangering rare plants and animal species – orang-utans face extinction – but deforestation also has a very negative impact on the carbon balance. Forests lock up carbon in their wood, and trap more of it in the humus and soil of the forest floor. Much of this is released when the land is cleared and burnt before planting with crops. In environmental terms, if you are going to clear forests to make bio-diesel, you might just as well use fossil fuel.

Fuel cells

The technology of fuel cells is very complex. For our purposes, it is enough to know that in the best types of fuel cell, hydrogen and oxygen are combined over a catalyst to produce electricity, and the only waste products are heat and water.

Fuel cells can be used wherever electricity is needed, but probably their most important use nowadays is as the 'engine' in cars. A fuel cell system of about the same size as an internal combustion engine will deliver enough electricity to power a car. And it will deliver up to 3 times more miles per gallon!

So why don't we all use fuel cell cars? The answer is that they are not yet on sale – but production models are expected soon. They will almost certainly be more expensive than the equivalent conventional car, but should be cheaper to run – mainly because they use fuel more efficiently, but there will also be tax and congestion charge benefits.

Hydrogen is the most efficient and cleanest fuel for fuel cells, but it's not the most convenient. The main problem is storage – you have to compress or liquefy it to fit a viable quantity into a reasonable space.

Electric (battery) cars

Battery-powered electric cars have been touted as the answer to urban transport for many years, but have only really taken off in the last couple of years. Tax incentives in several countries, such as exemption from London's congestion charge, have stimulated the market, and improvements in battery design mean that electric cars are a practical alternative to internal combustion ones for city driving. Modern electric cars, like the G-Wiz, can zip around through traffic with the same acceleration as most normal cars. (And the top speed of around 45 mph is not a problem in town.)

An overnight charge costs around 40p (at off-peak rates) and will power the car for up to 40 miles – that's right, about 1p a mile!

Electric cars are not without environmental impact – batteries pose the biggest problem. A standard battery has a life of three years, after which it must be replaced and disposed of. There is a new generation of lithium batteries just coming onto the market. These promise twice the lifespan, twice the power storage, and simpler disposal.

Most of the electric cars currently on the market are designed to be one-person run-arounds. They will take a second person and the shopping, but not much more – ideal for commuters, but not a practical family vehicle. The Mega City also comes in a 2+2 version, which could take the children (while they are small).

At first sight, electric cars can seem to be expensive compared with other small cars. They cost upwards of £8,000 new and the batteries will set you back £1,500 every three years. Against that, you have a running cost saving of at least 7p per mile, no congestion charge or road tax (and cheap/free parking in London). In London, an electric car can pay for itself completely in a couple of years – mainly because of the congestion charge exemption and parking concessions. Elsewhere, an electric car is not the cheapest solution to urban travel, though it is the greenest.

Which car?

If you decide that you do need a car, which one is right for you? Focus on how the car will be used most of the time.

* How many people will normally be travelling in it?
* How much luggage will it be carrying?
* How often will it be used to transport bulky loads?

Remember the mantra:

* **Small is beautiful** – Pick the smallest car that will do the job most of the time.
* **Least is best** – And sometimes leased is best. If you only need a large vehicle a few times a year, then perhaps you should buy a small one and hire a large one when needed.

* **Use and reuse** – Do you need a new car? Can you continue to use your existing one longer? Will a second-hand car do the job just as well?

Once you have decided on the type, there are several services on the web that will tell you the greenest of that type, and/or give you detailed figures of selected models. CO_2 emission levels and mpg figures are the two obvious measures of 'greenness', but they are not the only factors. The environmental impact of the car's construction is also an issue – for example, how much recycled material is used in making it and how easily can it be recycled at the end of its life. **What Green Car** (www.whatgreencar.com) includes fuel, emissions and the vehicle life cycle in its assessments to produce their guide to greener car buying.

Air travel

Over the last half-century, air travel has grown more than twice as fast as average economic growth, and this trend is expected to continue into the foreseeable future, with passenger numbers set to double by 2020. Currently, air travel is estimated to be responsible for about 5 per cent of the world's greenhouse gas emissions – as much as is generated by all human activity in Africa! This is projected to triple to 15 per cent by 2050 as air travel increases while other forms of pollution are brought under control.

Flight is the most environmentally damaging form of travel. A round trip from the UK to Australia generates – per passenger – as much CO_2 as is produced in heating and lighting the average house for a whole year. Short-haul flights are proportionately worse (it takes more energy to get up than to stay up). Compared with using the car (with one occupant), flying is five times as damaging; compared with taking the train, it does ten times more damage.

Carbon-offset schemes

Carbon offsetting is presented as the guilt-free way to fly. The theory is simple. When you are booking your flight, you pay a little extra which will be contributed to a project that will in some way reduce the amount of CO_2 in the atmosphere by the same amount that your flight will put into it. And voila, carbon-neutral flying! It's the same principle that is used in emissions trading, where large-scale polluters buy into reforestation, renewable energy development or similar schemes.

There have been some doubts about their effectiveness and value.

It's interesting that the Co-op's travel business, Travelcare, having announced its carbon-offset facility at the start of 2007, had abandoned it by the end of the same year.

Must-do

* Support any campaigns against new runways and for taxes on flights.
* Fly less, or stop flying altogether.

Worth doing

* **Take the train** – At one-tenth of the CO_2 emissions of a flight, this is the most environmentally friendly way to travel. Eurostar will take you from London to Paris at an environmental cost of 5.5 kg of CO_2 – a flight would cost 50 kg.
* **Switch to virtual business meetings** – Teleconferencing is a practical alternative to travel for business meetings. Presentations and documents can be shared and worked on collaboratively through internet connections.

Tourism

Most forms of tourism are environmentally damaging. We burn up oil by the air mile getting there; stay in concrete hotels that took large quantities of energy and resources to build and continue to take energy and resources to run; we play golf on courses that have wiped out eco-systems and draw masses of water from dwindling rivers and reservoirs; we destroy the local culture and replace it with standard holiday facilities; the tour operators and hotel chains employ locals on minimum wages and export the profits back to the West. It doesn't have to be this way.

Ecotourism

Ecotourism has been the fastest-growing sector of the tourism industry over the last few years, and now accounts for around 5 per cent of all holidays. It's an unfortunate fact that many of the environmentally aware, ecologically oriented holidays are in distant lands, so there are a lot of air miles travelled in reaching them – which creates something of a dilemma.

Ecotourism is environmentally friendly travel – going to natural areas in a way that helps to protect the environment and improves the lot of the local inhabitants. It is used by many countries to help finance the protection of the natural environment. For most, it is a fairly marginal activity, but there are some where ecotourism makes a very significant contribution to the total economy.

Some activities that are promoted as ecotourism hardly meet these criteria, and the 'eco' label is not much more than 'greenwashing' (making things appear to be more environmentally friendly than they really are). You will find, for example, safaris labelled 'ecotourism' that involve internal flights, extensive 4 × 4 driving and accommodation in (energy-intensive) luxury hotels.

Sustainable tourism

'Take nothing but pictures, leave nothing but footprints and waste nothing but time.'

Sustainable tourism aims to preserve the local environment, society and economy, so that future tourists can enjoy them and so that the locals continue to get a benefit from tourism. It's about working with the local people to provide low-impact activities, low-energy accommodation, and low-carbon travel, and ensuring that a large part of the profits stay in the local area.

The most sustainable tourism, of course, is that which requires the least travel. Holidays in the UK, or those reached by ferry and car on the nearer parts of the continent, must be better. A holiday which involves little travel once you have arrived will also be better. In fact, the most environmentally responsible holidays are probably the ones like those that most people took in the not too distant past – by train to the seaside.

Must-do

* Give the planet a break. Resist the lures of cheap weekend flights to Dublin, Barcelona and Rome. If you want to get away for the weekend, take the train – there are lots of interesting places in the UK, and Paris is only two and a half hours from central London nowadays.
* Give yourself a break from driving. Even if you have to use the car to get there, aim to keep out of the car as far as possible while you are on holiday. Walk and cycle to get around – you don't have to be anywhere in a hurry because you are on holiday.

Worth doing

* Choose locally owned, low-impact accommodation in preference to high-rise, high maintenance hotels owned by international chains.
* Think about ecotourism for your next holiday (preferably at a destination you can reach without flying).

Notes

Notes